THE INDO-SUMERIAN SEALS DECIPHERED

DISÇOVERING SUMERIANS OF INDUS VALLEY AS PHOENICIANS, BARATS, GOTHS & FAMOUS VEDIC ARYANS 3100-2300 B.C

THE INDO-SUMERIAN SEALS DECIPHERED

DISCOVERING SUMERIANS OF INDUS VALLEY AS PHOENICIANS, BARATS, GOTHS & FAMOUS VEDIC ARYANS 3100-2300 B.C

BY

L. A. WADDELL
LL.D., C.B., C.I.E.

Fellow of the Royal Anthropological Institute, Linnean and Folk-Lore Societies, Hon. Correspondt. Indian Archaeological Survey, Ex-Professor of Tibetan, London University

WITH NUMEROUS ILLUSTRATIONS AND MAPS

GYAN

Published by

Gyan Publishing House
5, Ansari Road
Daryaganj, New Delhi-110002
Phone: 011-47034999, 9811692060
E-mail: books@gyanbooks.com

Distribution Network
gyanbooks.com
India, USA, Canada, UK, Australia, France

ISBN : 978-81-212-2508-3 (HB)
First Published, 1925

2nd Impression 2021

Printed at: Gyan Press, Delhi.

The
Indo-Sumerian Seals Deciphered
Author: L. A. Waddell

THE INDO-SUMERIAN SEALS DECIPHERED

DISCOVERING SUMERIANS OF INDUS VALLEY AS PHŒNICIANS, BARATS, GOTHS & FAMOUS VEDIC ARYANS

3100-2300 B.C.

BY

L. A. WADDELL

LL.D., C.B., C.I.E.

Fellow of the Royal Anthropological Institute, Linnean and Folk-Lore Societies, Hon. Correspondt. Indian Archæological Survey, Ex-Professor of Tibetan, London University

WITH NUMEROUS ILLUSTRATIONS AND MAPS

LONDON

LUZAC & CO.

46 GREAT RUSSELL STREET, W.C.

1925

PLATE I. (*Frontispiece*).

Victory " seal " of (A-)Madgal (Mudgala), " Lord of Indus Valley " (Edin), Sumerian crown-prince of Mesopotamia about 3070 B.C.

From contemporary " seal " in Louvre Museum.

(After M. Delaporte (D.C.O. T. 98). By kind permission of Librairie Hachette.) *See pp.* 34 *f*.

PREFACE

In my recent work on British Origins, I proved by a mass of new historical evidence that the "Sumerians"—those foremost civilized and civilizing ancient people whose monuments and high art of five thousand years ago are the wonder of the modern world—were the long lost Early Aryans; that the Phœnicians were not Semites as has been hitherto supposed, but Aryans and the chief colonizing branch of the Sumerians; and that the people who colonized and civilized India, as well as those who colonized and civilized the Mediterranean, North-western Europe and Britain and who were the ancestors of the Britons, were likewise Aryan and belonged predominantly to the Phœnician branch of that race.

These results are now dramatically confirmed, both as regards India and the British Isles, by the discovery in the Indus Valley, a few weeks after the publication of my book, of two large series of ancient seals inscribed with Sumerian writing, unearthed from beneath the foundations of old Buddhist buildings of the third century B.C., to the second century A.D., at widely different sites on the Indus, and associated with the ancient buildings and tombs of the owners of the seals, and cultural objects of ancient Sumerian and Phœnician type.

That the writing on these seals was "Sumerian" and of an archaic type I recognized on the first glance at their photographs; and I found later that Professor Sayce and other Assyriologists had arrived at the like conclusion, but that owing to the writing being slightly different from the straight-lined script of the clay tablets, they had been unable to read a single word of the inscriptions on the seals.

On the other hand, having in my search for Aryan Origins been led by various clues to the conclusion that the Sumerians were Aryans, and devoted a great part of the last twenty years to the study of the ancient Sumerian writing at first hand, the problem of the Indus Valley script was to me a comparatively easy one. So much so that within a day or two of receiving the photographs I was able—and I say so without any wish to boast—to decipher and read the greater part of the inscriptions on the seals. The subsequent weeks before going to press have been spent in revising the decipherments—which are now believed to be substantially correct—and in ransacking the Vedas and Indian Epics for the detailed references to the various famous Aryan Vedic kings, princes and priests whose names are inscribed on the seals.

The owners of several of these Sumerian seals, I soon observed, bore the names of famous Vedic Aryan seers and princes with whom I had become familiar in the Vedic hymns of the Brahmans, and some of whom were specified therein as living on the banks of the Indus. Most of the others, for fortunately all the seals are engraved with their owners' names with one exception, are identified with other Vedic and Epic Aryan heroes who are disclosed as governors of a colony of seafaring Sumerian or Phœnician merchants and exploiters of the mineral wealth of the Indus Valley, and through the Ravi tributary of the latter the gold-fields of Tibet from about 3100 B.C.

The colony was founded by the famous Sumerian king of that epoch, Uruas', the Haryas'wa of the Vedas and Indian Epics, and the " Ur Nina " of Assyriologists, who is generally regarded as the first great dynast of the Early Sumerians ; and he is now disclosed to be a Phœnician, the founder of the First Dynasty of Phœnicians in Mesopotamia, and the son of the great Hercules of the Phœnicians and Greeks, here conclusively identified with the Sumerian epic hero " Gilgamesh " of Erech, and now disclosed for the first time as a historical human Aryan Sumerian Phœnician king and great Sun-priest of Bel of relatively fixed date, about 3150 B.C.

The seals are in fact the official signets and grave-amulets of the administrators with their family priests of a Mesopotamian colony in the distant Indus Valley whose very existence had been hitherto unsuspected by Assyriologists. Some of them are the official signets of famous historical Sumerian and " Akkad " kings of Mesopotamia as suzerains of the colony, including Sargon I, who appears to have personally visited it. And the seals extend down to the end of the Ur Dynasty about 2350 B.C., on the overthrow of that dynasty by its tributary province of Elam, when they suddenly cease, presumably owing to the colony having been lost to Mesopotamia and abandoned.

All these Sumerian and " Akkad " kings, governors and priests are duly recorded in the Vedas and Indian Epics as " Aryans " ; and some of them are called " The able *Panch* " which I have shown is a form of " Phœnic-ian." On their Indus Valley seals, several bear the title of " Aryan " and of " Phœnician " by its more common synonyms, and others call themselves " Amorite," Goth and " Scyth," thus confirming my discoveries announced in the former work that the Sumerians, " Akkads," Amorites and Phœnicians were racially Aryans. Moreover, they use on their grave-amulet seals the same Sumerian sacred numeral script or " cup-mark " script, and couched in substantially the same formulas to the Sun-god as I have shown in my former work, were used by the Early Sumerians, Phœnicians, Amorites and Trojans, and by the Early Britons on their " cup-marked " tombs in Ancient Britain, and thus confirming my reading of this cup-mark script on the British monuments, and the Phœnician origin of the Britons.

At the same time it is made clear that these early Aryan Sumero-Phœnicians who established and kept this colony on the Indus for about eight centuries, did not form a part of that great Aryan immigration which is now generally called " The Aryan Invasion of India." This latter event, with its permanent occupation and systematic civilization of the heart of India, the Ganges Valley or Hindustan, I find from a mass of new evidence, took place no earlier than the beginning of the seventh century B.C., and not by sea, but overland from Asia Minor and Syria-Phœnicia, through Persia and across the Lower Indus, by a remnant of the Hittite army and Aryan Syrio-Phœnician people seeking new settlements after their calamitous defeat by the Assyrian Sargon II at Carchemish in 718 B.C.

The unique authenticity of the Indian Epic king-lists, as an independent source of Sumerian and Mesopotomian history—a discovery announced in my former work—is now strikingly confirmed by the evidence of these seals. The official Hittite origin of these king-lists, as the traditional lists of the Aryan kings from the Hittite archives back to the first Aryan dynasty in prehistoric times, and the circumstances which led to their being embedded and preserved in the Indian Epics by the Hitto-Sumerian remnant of the Aryans on their exodus to India about 700 B.C.; and my discovery that the ancient Aryan kings were Sumerians are set forth in my previous work. These Indian king-lists are now found to preserve systematically the ancestry and interrelations of the leading Mesopotamian kings and dynasties, with the original form of their names for the period of these seals, as also of antecedent and subsequent periods, which while in part disclosed by the Sumerian monuments, are still in great part unknown or misknown to Assyriologists, dependent as they are on isolated and fragmentary records and late Semitic, Chaldean and alien king-lists.

But the most fatal practical defect in the methods of Assyriologists disclosed by the comparison of these Indian king-list keys with the seals and with the Sumerian monuments and king-lists is that *a great proportion of the names of Sumerian and Babylonian kings, gods and places, as "restored" by Assyriologists is largely and often wholly fictitious;* and thus has been misleading the public and students of comparative history and religion, by disguising the personalities and racial and linguistic affinities of the Sumerians.

This inveterate defect in the restoration of the personal and place names of Sumerians by Assyriologist scholars is now seen to have arisen through the ambiguities of Sumerian being an *imperial* or cosmopolitan composite language, which incorporated many foreign words borrowed from the diverse speech of the many subject non-Aryan races and tribes of the Sumerian empire. For the Sumerian scribes for the most part wrote their loan-words by the same picto-graphic word-sign as bore their Sumerian sound-values, from which it resulted that the selfsame word-sign in Sumerian syllabic writing usually possesses in the glossaries many different polyglottic (so-called " polyphonous ") values, often half a dozen or more, with no indication as to which was the pure Sumerian (*i.e.*, Aryan) value. Hence Assyriol-ogists in " restoring " the spelling of a Sumerian proper name from its polyglottic syllabic signs into alphabetic spelling, and possessing no clue or notion whatever as to what the real phonetic form of that name was (except in a few instances where the glossaries give an unequivocal spelling), they are in the habit of selecting any one of these totally different phonetic values *by mere guesswork*, each scholar according to his own individual fancy. As a con-sequence the names thus coined at random by Assyriologists from the selfsame Sumerian word-signs are as bizarre as they are varied and so often fictitious.

The result of finding such vagaries in the " restored " spelling of the selfsame Sumerian name by Assyriologists and the haphazard cause of the same, is to dissipate all faith in the form of proper names so " restored." For unless the Sumerian syllabic word-sign chances fortunately to possess but one phonetic value, and thus cannot be varied, which is seldom, no confidence whatever can be placed on the form and spelling of the names thus conjectur-ally restored.

Now, however, this fatal defect in restoring Sumerian proper names of leading kings, priests and gods, is remedied to a great extent by our Indian Epic lists of the Early Aryan kings and dynasties. These place in our hands the traditional official lists of the names of those ancestral Aryan kings and dynasties, who we find were the Sumerian and " Akkad " kings of Early Mesopotamia, with their names in the phonetic form known to and preserved by their lineal

Aryan descendants. And these names for the period of these seals, as we shall see, are in substantial agreement with those inscribed on the seals and on their own monuments in Mesopotamia, although in most cases differing widely from those as hitherto conjecturally " restored " by Assyriologists. *These Indian Epic king-lists are thus found to provide, as far as they go, a unique and the only known key to the restoration of the proper names and titles of the Sumerian and " Akkad " kings of Mesopotamia.*

A striking example of the invaluable practical use of these Indian Epic king-lists in recovering the true and original form of the names and titles of Sumerian kings is furnished by its preservation of the kings' names of the First Dynasty of Phœnicians, which founded the Indus Valley colony and some of whose seals are figured. This dynasty, hitherto considered the first concrete dynasty of the Early Sumerians, and founded by the famous " Ur-Nina," was so great, that its galaxy of inscribed monuments, sculptures, seals and other works of art and craft, and massive buildings, temples and store-houses, unearthed at Telloh (" Lagash "), " the Pompeii of Early Mesopotamian antiquity," by M. de Sarzec during a quarter of a century, from 1877 to 1900, still forms the chief basis of our knowledge of the Early Sumerians. And it is actually taken as such by Professor Langdon in his recent historical sketch of the Sumerians in the *Cambridge Ancient History*, no further back than in 1923. Nevertheless, a few months later, in the *same* year, that Assyriologist, on finding a legendary list of Mesopotamian kings written by credulous priests of the petty and supposed alien dynasty at Isin, over a thousand years after the epoch of " Ur Nina," and purporting to give a complete list of the kings with their regnal years back to 241,200 years before the Flood (!), accepts such a semi-fabulous list seriously, in preference to the sober testimony of the contemporary records of the historical Sumerian kings on their own monuments. And, merely because he could not find in this Isin list either the name " Ur Nina," or those of the rest of his dynasty, or indeed of nearly all the other historical Sumerian kings, including the famous and prolific emperor

Gudea, whose existing monuments make up nearly the sum-total of known Sumerian history, he throws over all these solidly-known historical kings with their monuments, and declares that they were mere impostors in calling themselves "kings" and dynasties—solely because he could not find them in his Isin list! And in this extraordinary conclusion Professor Sayce also has agreed.

But other Assyriologists may now be reassured. That inference from the Isin list is merely "a mare's nest." Not only are "Ur Nina" and his dynasty all there, I find, but they are made even in this Isin list the first of all "human" Sumerian dynasties in Mesopotamia, as we shall find through the Indian king-lists, though their names and titles were not recognized by the professors, mainly through having "restored" the names mostly with the wrong phonetic values. And thus one at least of the several extra thousands of years which these scholars have generously added to the date of the Sumerians in Mesopotamia, before Ur Nina's epoch, on the strength of their reading of this list, has now got to be removed again.

It is far from pleasant for me, indebted as I am for most of my knowledge of "Sumerian" to the labours of a great body of expert scholars, to be forced to expose these serious defects in their methods and theories which stand in the way of recovering true history. But no one should be more aware of the existence of these defects than themselves. And I trust that the means now offered for remedying them will receive that fair and impartial consideration, without which it is idle to hope for any advance in our knowledge of history.

"Sumerian," of course, is not found written on any of these seals, for this is merely another of those misleading labels which Assyriologists have arbitrarily affixed to this Aryan race. It has never once been found employed by these people themselves, nor has the word ever been found in any "Sumerian" inscription or document, yet the public have been led, or rather misled, to believe that it was the genuine name of this pre-eminently civilized ancient Aryan people. Nor is the use by Assyriologists of the associated

Semitic name "Akkad" any better. That name they now apply to their hypothetical "Western Semites" (who, we find, were Aryans), and use it to distinguish these from the decidedly non-Semitic "Sumerians"; although some years ago Professor Sayce and others habitually used it in the diametrically opposite sense, applying it to the people whom they now term "Sumerians" and *vice versa*. That name, however, is merely a Semitic term for the land called by Sumerians *Ari-ki* or *Uri-ki*, *i.e.*, "Land of the *Ari* or Aryans"—a land the exact site of which is not yet known, but which Assyriologists suppose to be in Upper Mesopotamia, because Sargon I, whom they have dubbed a "Western Semite," called his capital "Agade," though he never uses the term "Akkad," nor is it found in the glossaries as a synonym for "Agade."

Among the many Vedic priests and kings whose historic personalities and in part bodily relics, seals and jewellery are thus recovered and identified are Ausija (Kakshivan) Kanwa, possibly Gautam Rishi himself, and certainly "the slave-girl" Usij, the reputed consort of the latter in the epic romance. Among the kings whose historic identities and dates and monuments are now recovered, are Haryas'wa with his father and grandfather, and his descendants of the Pānch-āla or Phœnician Dynasty, including especially Mudgala with his Indus Valley seal and famous stone-maces (?), Badhryas'wa and Dīvo-Dāsa, the emperor Sakuni or Sagara, the priest kings Gādhi, Jamadagni, Sushena and the truculent Parās'u Rāma.

For the Hindus and students of Indian history, civilization and religion therefore, these discoveries must be of especial thrilling interest and importance. They disclose the actual official signets and grave-amulets of several of the most famous Vedic seers and authors of Vedic hymns, and of ancient kings and heroes whose very existence even is denied by European Sanskrit scholars, with the actual tombs of many of them containing their sacred dust. And with these are recovered for the first time the actual dates and reigns in which they lived four to five thousand years ago. We also recover through their identifications the authentic portraits of many of them from their own contemporary seals and monuments, vividly portraying their features and dress. Some of these portraits are given in the frontispiece and text, and many others in my *Origin of the Indo-Aryans*. As most of the seals were exhumed from the actual tombs of the saints and heroes named on the seals at their ancient Phœnician Sun-temples, these Indus Valley sites will doubtless now become popular places of Hindu pilgrimage. And it is to be hoped that the priceless seals and historical relics of these illustrious Early Aryan pioneers will be suitably safeguarded.

On the origin of the Brahmanist and Vedic religion also, much fresh historical light is shed by the seals. The early Vedic religion is disclosed as apparently a monotheism with the Sumerian Induru—the Sanskrit Indra—as the "enthroned" Father-god, with his beneficent Sun-angel Vishnu (the so-called Ninā of the Assyriologists), who also assumes the dual or twin form of the Nāsatya or Day and Night or "Resurrecting" Sun, who is invoked for Resurrection from the Dead; and it is noteworthy that there is no trace of goddesses. The Sumerian origin and meaning of these god-names, and of the Fish "incarnation" (avatar) of Vishnu are disclosed for the first time—this Fish form of the Sun-angel being also found to be the Sumero-Phœnician source of the names as well as representations of the Greek and Roman sea-god Poseidon or Neptune, the *Napat* of the Vedas. There is also disclosed the Sumerian origin and meaning of the priestly titles "Brahman" and "Bhrigu"; the concrete evidence for the Kshattriyas or "warrior or ruling caste" having been the first Brahmans; and for the exaltation of the Brahmans to the first caste by Parās'u Rāma with exact dates for these events.

The discoveries herein recorded should therefore appeal to the hearts and stir the religious and patriotic feelings of all educated Hindus who desire to know the first-found scientific proofs for the veracity of their Vedas and Ancient Epics (the Purānas), and to learn that their ancestral Vedic kings and sages were famous historical emperors, kings and priest-kings in Mesopotamia with multitudinous monuments still existing there to the present day. It must also be gratifying to the modern Hindus to find that the Vedic and Epic tradition which their ancestors preserved and handed down through the centuries, and in which they have steadfastly believed, is now proved substantially true, and has become a chief means of identifying as Aryans, the Sumerians, Phœnicians and Britons.

Besides this, it is now proved that the ancient Vedic sages and kings and people wrote and spoke in the "Sumerian" tongue—a language which is now disclosed to be the parent Aryan speech, the parent of the Sanskrit, Hindi, Marāthā, Bengali, and the other Aryan dialects of India, as well as of Europe and especially of the British or "English." Several instances of this are given in these pages, in addition to those in my former work, with reference to critical words incidentally occurring; but from an extensive survey I have found that over fifty per cent. of the basic words in Sanskrit and Hindi as in Old English are clearly derived from the Sumerian. On this account, and also because the vast collection of Sumerian Hymns doubtless contain original versions of many Vedic hymns, it behoves Indianists and Sanskritists, as well as the British to commence the study of "Sumerian," in view of the new vistas thus opened up for Aryans.

For the British people, these discoveries are of prime historical importance as by confirming and further establishing the Aryan and non-Semitic origin of the Phœnicians, and their authorship of the "cup-mark" inscriptions with similar formulas on the tombs of the Early Britons, they confirm the Phœnician ancestry of the Britons as established in my former work. Thus the evidence of these seals gives fresh ground for patriotism in the glory of descent of the Britons from the originators of the Worlds' Higher Civilization, and the foremost adventurous seamen of the Ancient World.

It would be affectation to ignore that in this and in the companion volume on British Origins, led by the new facts, I am in opposition to much of what is held to be, if not established doctrine, at any rate good working theory with regard to Sumerian, Phœnician, Indian and British history. I am also at variance with both general and expert opinion as regards the nature and causes of the so-called "Higher Civilization." I take the phrase to mean, not, as a visitor to the earth from Mars might suppose, aeroplanes and motors, telephones and wireless, athletics and gambling, trashy books, novels and newspapers, and a religion based largely on myths and réchauffés of the rites and superstitions of savages; but briefly, art, science and a healthy contented populace.

And as regards Origins, I find myself opposed not merely to the theorists who trace most of our culture to Judaism; but also to those who refer it to an effect, manifested rather suddenly some six thousand years ago, of the Egyptian climate on the mixed populations who at that period inhabited the Nile Valley; and also to those who look upon Civilization as arising independently amongst different races at different centres and due to a supposedly widely distributed similar temperamental strain amongst different races reacting in the very same way when exposed to the same circumstances in the early historic and later prehistoric times.

I have great pleasure in acknowledging again my indebtedness to my friend Dr Islay Burns Muirhead, M.A., for helpful criticism and remarks on some of the leading inferences. And I must express my thanks to The Edinburgh Press for the exceptional care they have bestowed on the printing of the book, with its accented oriental names and the detailed footnotes, necessary for the full authentication of the facts.

L. A. WADDELL.

April, 1925.

FIG. A.—Izzax (Gis'zax), king of Erek about 3150 B.C., or "'Erakles," father of Uruas' (Sanskrit *Haryas'wa*), "King of Indus Valley" and founder of First Phœnician Dynasty, slaying the Lion.

(From a Sumerian seal of about 2600 B.C. in British Museum.)

Note the trees or reeds of (Nemean?) grove. On right the hero is crushing the lion, and on left is lifting the dead beast. For proofs identifying this Erek King as the Sumerian human source of Hercules of the Phœnicians, Greeks and Romans, see App. V.

CONTENTS

APPENDICES

FIG. B.—Izzax, king of Erek about 3150 B.C. and father of founder of Indus colony, slaying the Lion and overpowering the mad Bull, *disclosing Sumerian historical source of 'Ĕrakles.*

(From seal of a "*Haryas'wa,*" about 2600 B.C., in British Museum, W.S.C., 168.)

LIST OF ILLUSTRATIONS

FIGURES IN TEXT

MAPS

ERRATA.

p. viii. l. 7 for Mesopotomian read *Mesopotamian*.

p. 26. In Fig. description for Tellsh read *Telloh.*

p. 51 ll. 7, 16 and 27, and p. 92 for Gim read *Gin.*

ABBREVIATIONS

FOR CHIEF REFERENCES

A.I.B.	Académie des Inscript. et Belles Lettres, Comptes Rendus, Paris.
A.R.V.	Hymen des Rig Veda. T. Aufrecht, Bonn, 1877.
A.S.I.	Archæological Survey Reports of India.
A.V.	Atharva Veda Samhitā. W. D. Whitney, Cambridge, Mass., U.S.A., 1905.
B.	Classified List of Cuneiform Ideographs. R. E. Brunnow, Leyden, 1889.
B.D.	Brihad-Devatā. A. A. Macdonell, Cambridge, Mass., U.S.A., 1904.
B.H.T.	Buddhist Records of Western World, translated from Chinese of Hiuen Tsiang. S. Beal, 1884.
B.I.M.	Mammalia of British India. W. T. Blanford, 1891.
B.M.C.	Cappadocian Tablets in British Museum. Pt. I., 1921.
B.W.	Babylonian Writing. G. A. Barton, Leipzig, 1913.
C.A.	Empire of the Amorites. A. T. Clay, New Haven, U.S.A., 1919.
C.D.N.	Documents from Temple Archives of Nippur. A. T. Clay, Philadelphia, 1906.
C.H.I.	Cambridge History of India, I., 1922.
C.J.	Jātakas transl. by E. B. Cowell, 1895–1913.
C.M.C.	Mission en Cappadoce. E. Chantre, Paris, 1898.
Cp.	Compare.
C.T.	Cuneiform Texts in British Museum.
D.C.O.	Cylindres Orientaux du Musée du Louvre. L. Delaporte, Librairie Hachette, Paris, 1923.
D.C.O.(B.)	Cylindres Orient. de la Bibliot. Nationale. L. Delaporte, Paris, 1910.
Déc.	Découvertes en Chaldée. E. de Sarzec et L. Heuzey, Paris.
G.H.V.	Hymns of Rig Veda, tr. by R. T. Griffiths, Benares, 1896.
H.	Herodotus.
H.C.	Carchemish. D. Hogarth, 1914.
H.H.S.	Hittite Seals. D. Hogarth, 1920.
I.A.	Indian Antiquary, Bombay.
J.A.O.S.	Journal of American Oriental Society, New Haven, U.S.A.
J.A.S.B.	Journal Asiatic Society of Bengal, Calcutta.
J.R.A.S.	Journal Royal Asiatic Society.
K.C.B.	Chronicles Early Babylonian Kings. L. W. King, 1907.
K.H.S.	History of Sumer and Akkad. L. W. King, 1916.
L.N.	Monuments of Nineveh. A. H. Layard.
L.S.G.	Sumerian Grammar. S. Langdon, Paris, 1911.
M.	Seltene assyrische Ideogramme. Meissner.
M.B.	Mahā-Bhārata. Calcutta text and English tr. by P. C. Roy (R.), Calcutta, 1893.
M.C.	Law Code of Manu.
M.D.	Dictionary of Assyrian Language. W. Muss-Arnolt, Berlin, 1905.

M.K.I.	Vedic Index. A. A. Macdonell and A. B. Keith, 1912.
M.R.	Report on First Light on a Long Forgotten Civilization, in *Illustrated London News*, pp. 528 f., Sept. 20, 1924. J. Marshall.
M.V.M.	Vedic Mythology. A. A. Macdonell, 1897.
M.W.D.	Sanskrit Dictionary. M. Monier-Williams, 1899.
P.A.B.	Coins of Cunobelin and Ancient Britain. B. Poste, 1853.
P.I.	Ancient Indian Hist. Tradition. F. E. Pargiter, 1922.
P.S.B.A.	Proc. Society of Biblical Archæology.
R.B.	Early Babylonian History. H. Radau, New York, 1900.
R.I.	Indus Delta Country. Raverty, 1894.
R.V.	Rig Veda.
S.	Sumerian.
S.B.	S'atapatha Brāhmana.
S.D.P.	Délégation en Perse. Mémoires Textes. V. Scheil, Paris, 1904, etc.
S.H.I.	Early History of India. V. A. Smith, 1908.
Skt.	Sanskrit.
St.	Strabo.
T.D.	Recherches sur l'origine de l'Ecriture Cunéiforme. F. Thureau-Dangin, Paris, 1898–9.
T.D.I.	Les Inscriptions Sumer et d'Akkad. F. Thureau-Dangin, Paris, 1905.
Va.	Vayu Purāna.
V.D.	Icelandic-English Dictionary. G. Vigfusson, 1874.
V.N.	Voyage of Nearchus. W. Vincent, 1797.
W.B.T.	The Buddhism of Tibet. L. A. Waddell, 1895.
W.E.P.	Excavations at Pataliputra (Patna). L. A. Waddell, Calcutta, 1903.
W.H.	Empire of the Hittites. W. Wright, 1886.
W.P.O.B.	Phœnician Origin of the Britons, Scots, and Anglo-Saxons. L. A. Waddell, 1924.
W.S.C.	Seal Cylinders of W. Asia. W. H. Ward, Washington, 1900.
W.V.P.	Vishnu Purāna, tr. by H. H. Wilson, ed. F. Hall, 1864–70.

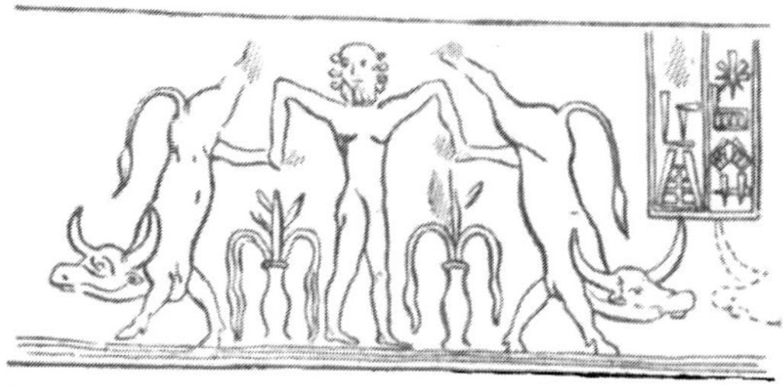

FIG. C.—Izzax, king of Erek about 3150 B.C., and father of Phœnician founder of Indus colony, cleansing the Oxen, *disclosing Sumerian historical source of 'Erakles* cleansing the Augean stables.

(From seal of about 2700 B.C., after Heuzey, W.S.C., 203.)

Note the *two* streams of water from spouting vase, representing the two rivers of the Greek legend (?). For details of identity see App. V.

THE
INDO-SUMERIAN SEALS DECIPHERED

I

Sumerian Origin of the Indo-Aryans and of their Civilization and Date of " Invasion "

> " The historian's duty is to separate the true from the false, the certain from the uncertain, and the doubtful from that which cannot be accepted."—Goethe, *Maxims*, No. 453.

In my recent book on " The Phœnician Origin of the Britons, Scots and Anglo-Saxons," I established by a mass of new historical evidence the unsuspected facts that the " Sumerians " were the long lost Early Aryans in race, speech and script ; that their chief seafaring and colonizing branch was the Hitto-Phœnician, including the Amorites and Kassi or Cassi ; and that the Indo-Aryans who conquered, colonized and civilized India, as well as the Western branch of Aryans who colonized and civilized the Mediterranean, North-west Europe and the British Isles, were those leading sea-going branches of the Aryan Sumerians.

These conclusions are now dramatically confirmed, as regards India, by the discovery in the Indus Valley of a large number of ancient seals inscribed with Sumerian writing and associated with buildings and cultural objects of Sumerian and Phœnician type.

At the time of writing the above-cited book, no inscribed monuments or documents or cultural objects of a higher civilization had been found in any part of the Indian continent which could be dated before the fifth century B.C. Thus, in summarizing the results of archæological exploration in India, I wrote "nothing whatever of traces of civilization (*i.e.*, the higher civilization), apart from the rude Stone Circles, has ever been found by the scientifically-equipped Indian Archæological Survey Department in their more or less exhaustive excavations on the oldest reputed sites down to the virgin soil, during over half a century, which can be specifically dated to before 600 B.C."[1] At the same time, I drew attention to the evidence of a former Early Aryan Phœnician or "Amorite" presence in Non-Gangetic India, in the "prehistoric" Stone Circles which stand at the ancient mine-workings in the Deccan and *in the Upper Indus Valley.*[2]

This was written to explain the significant fact that in the Gangetic Valley—that is in the traditional centre of "*The* India" of the Brahmans with the Hindu Holy Land *par excellence*—Aryan Civilization of precisely the same kind which has persisted in that land down to modern times *suddenly appears in fully fledged form about* 650 B.C., in the pages of Brahmanist Epics and Buddhist literature, thus suggesting that the so-called "Aryan Invasion of India" with its permanent occupation, colonization and systematic civilization of the heart of India, *i.e.*, the Ganges Valley or Hindustan, occurred at or about that epoch.

It was also to explain the other significant facts which I had elicited, that the Early Aryan kings of the Indian Vedas and the "Ancient Epics" (Purānas) with their multitudinous King-lists and Ancient Dynasties, reigned *not in India as was supposed but in Mesopotamia and Syria-Phœnicia or Hittite Asia Minor,* and were identical in names, successive order and exploits with well-known historical kings and emperors of the Sumerians and Hittites

[1] W.P.O.B., 15. [2] *Ib.*, 218, 223.

in Mesopotamia, Syria and Asia Minor, whose original inscribed monuments and official records still exist there and in the museums of Europe in vast numbers to the present day. It thus explained how the language and religion of the Indo-Aryans were, as I had elicited, radically identical with those of the Sumerians and Hitto-Phœnicians.

It moreover explained the direct connecting link which I had found, namely that the first semi-historical king of India, with his "Syria-Phœnician" followers, and his capital near Delhi in the Ganges Valley, under whom the first partition of India traditionally took place in the post-Vedic period, at the time of the Mahā-Bhārata War about 650 B.C., was the Bhārat *Khattiyo* king Dhrita-rashtra, *the last Aryan king mentioned in the Vedas*, and who is shown in the detailed Indian Epic King-lists to be *descended from those Early Aryan kings now found to be Sumerians*. And he was the Son of the *Khattiyo* "*Wicitra*—the hero" (Vicitra-virya) who, I found, was identical with, and had the same predecessors as, the *Khatti* (or "Hittite") king *Wi-si-di(ri)* who was the last Hittite king of Carchemish in Upper Mesopotamia, and slain by the Semitic Assyrian king Sargon II in 718 B.C. All this indicated that while the Indo-Aryans were directly descended from the Sumerians, the so-called "Great Aryan Invasion of India," *i.e.*, of the Ganges Valley, occurred no earlier than about 700 B.C., and in the post-Vedic period.

After the MS. of that book was completed and ready for the press, I observed that two ancient seals were reported in 1922 as having been unearthed at Harappa on a chief tributary of the Indus above Mooltan, and inscribed in an "unknown pictographic script."[1] On seeing the photographs of these seals (see Fig. 1), I at once recognized the script as Sumerian and deciphered the inscriptions (see decipherment and translations at pp. 31, 40 f.) But as these seals related to the

[1] C.H.I., 617–8.

Indus Valley on the extreme western border of India, and *not* to the Ganges Valley, the reputed traditional centre of " Ancient Indian Civilization," and were merely " said to be found " at Harappa, and thus might have been brought there from Mesopotamia or Asia Minor, and as " The Land of Edin " mentioned in one of them was wholly unknown to Assyriologists, I did not notice these seals in that work which had already greatly outgrown its original dimensions and scope.

Even now, after deciphering these two seals, as well as the numerous others bearing this same Sumerian script, which were subsequently unearthed at Harappa and at another site on the Lower Indus, from the actual buildings and graves of their authors, and associated with many cultural objects of a Sumerian type, we shall find that although these seals, etc., contribute priceless concrete testimony to the former early presence of Sumerians in the Indus Valley, and identify them with Vedic Aryans, and attest their possession of river-ports or stations in the Indus Valley for nearly a thousand years, still in the absence of such finds elsewhere in India, and in the Ganges Valley in particular, they do not necessarily imply that these Early Sumerians of the Indus Valley were members or descendants of what is generally called " The Aryan Invasion of India "—that invasion which suddenly appeared and annexed and *permanently* ruled, colonized and civilized the whole of India, and in particular the Ganges Valley or Hindustan.

On the contrary, these Early Sumerians in the Indus Valley appear from the testimony of their own seals, etc. to have been merely an early temporary wave of Sumerian (*i.e.*, Vedic Aryan) seafaring traders who penetrated to the Indus Valley, and holding it as a colony of Mesopotamia settled there for several centuries accompanied by their families and family priests. They seem to have been an advance-guard, but transient, of the same Aryan Sumerian race which eventually came in greater force, overland through Persia from Upper Mesopotamia, Media and Asia Minor, and making their headquarters in the Ganges Valley permanently annexed and civilized India as the great so-

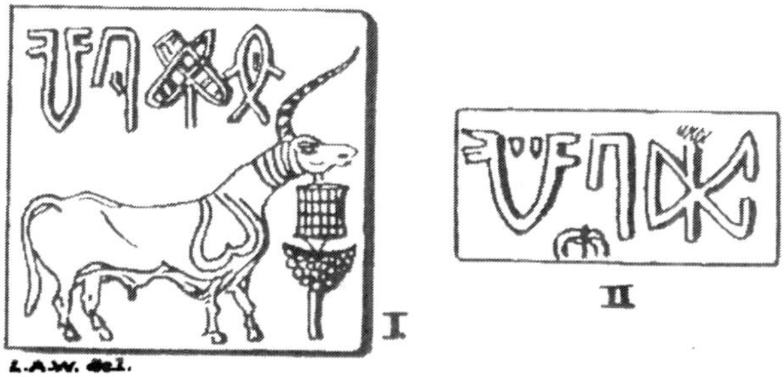

FIG. 1.—Sumerian Seals from Harappa in Upper Indus Valley (actual size). (After Camb. Anc. Hist. India.)[1]

called "Aryan Invasion of India." They thus appear to afford an early instance of that peaceful penetration by seafaring Aryan merchants—a process not unknown in modern times—which after many centuries ultimately led up to the great "Aryan Invasion of India" by a later branch of the same "Sumerian" race, presumably about 700 B.C.

[1] C.H.I., pl. xi., 22–3.

II

Sites of the Indo-Sumerian Seals and associated buildings, etc., in Indus Valley with their Ancient History

Disclosing Place-Names on Seals as Ancient Indus River-ports of Phœnicians ; and " Indus " origin of name " India."

THE site where the first two " Sumerian " seals were " said to be " found is at Harappa,[1] above Mooltan, in the Montgomery District of the Panjab, on the left bank of the Ravi River, at or near an old junction with the Bias tributary of the Indus (see sketch-map). Other seals of the same type were subsequently unearthed during the excavation of the foundations of the Buddhist ruins surmounting the old site at Harappa by Mr. D. R. Sahni of the Indian Archæological Survey ; and the remainder by Mr. R. D. Banerji of the same department in excavating the foundations of the Buddhist ruins at Mohenjo Daro,[2] on the Lower Indus, in the Larkhana District of Sind, about 190 miles above the modern seaport of Karachi in the delta of the Indus (see map).

Now it is of immense importance for us to examine the ancient history and topography of these two sites, as far as is known, in some detail, especially as I find that *the place-name inscribed on most of these Sumerian seals preserves the original name of the ancient seaport and city-state of the Lower Indus, the name of which survived there down to the*

[1] C.H.I., 111. [2] M.R., 528.

seventh century of the Christian era. There is the further interest that one, if not both, of these sites stand upon the classic route of Alexander, in his retreat down the Indus

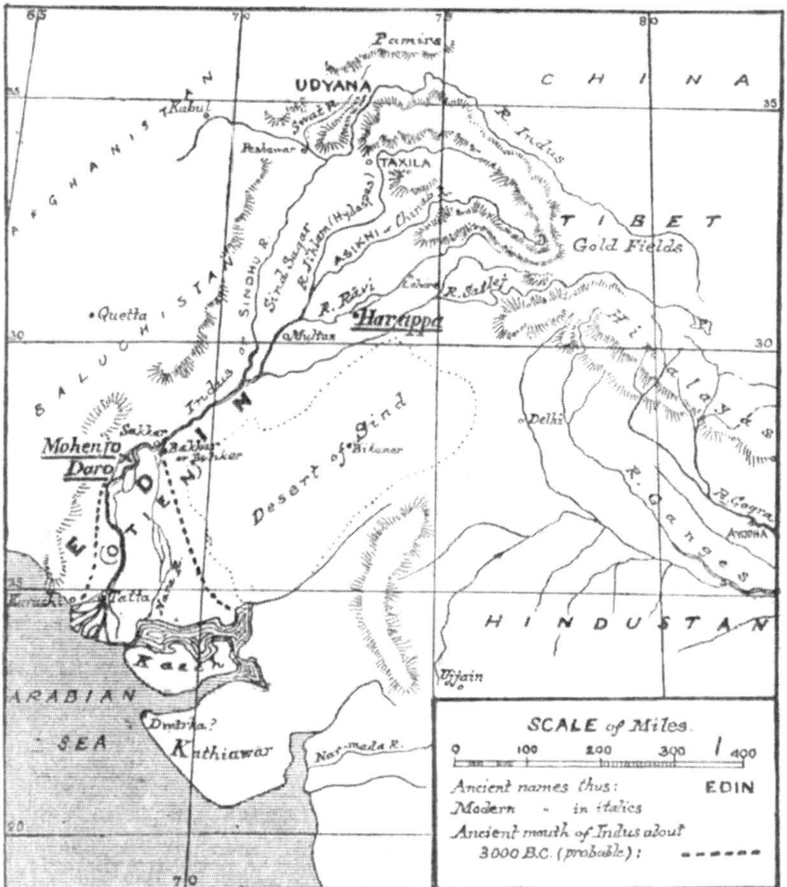

L.A.W. del.

Map of Indus Valley, showing "Find" sites of Seals.

from its tributary Jhelam (Hydaspes), from his attempted conquest of India 326–325 B.C. And Alexander's historians have recorded many important details regarding the places and tribes in the neighbourhood of both these sites.

At the outset, it is noteworthy that the Indus Valley, which is referred to several times in the Vedic hymns as exploited by Early Aryan *Marutas* (or Amorites) [1] and *Krivi* (or Syrio-Phœnicians) [2] for its gold-dust and drugs, etc., was apparently until Alexander's invasion the sole "India" known to the early Greeks and the Persians.[3] And our modern name of "India" is derived from the name of the Indus River, the extension of that name to the Ganges Valley being post-Alexandrine, and its extension to the southern part of that peninsula of still much later date.

The Indus, under the name of Sindhu, is repeatedly mentioned in the Vedas as an especial abode of the *Maruta* (or Amorites) [4] "who rise from the sea, who abide in the sea." Thus the Maruta are invoked:

> "So let not . . . Sindhu hold you back." [5]

And they were defenders there of the *Krivi* (the Syrio-Phœnicians):

> "The Maruta are victorious and guard the Sindhu well,
> And succour the Krivi in his need." [6]

The Maruts also brought healing remedies from the Indus Valley and its upper tributary the Asikni (the Akesines of

[1] On *Maruta* of Sanskrit as the Sumerian *Maruta* or "Amorite" see my W.P.O.B., 216, 243, etc.

[2] On *Krivi* and *Kuru-Panch-āla* as "Syrio-Phœnician" *ib.*, 12, 13, 188, etc.

[3] H., 3, 98 f.; 4–44. Alexander, who never penetrated to the Ganges Valley, probably heard during his expedition of that richer and more populous valley; for his eastern satrap and successor Seleukos Nikator sent his ambassador Megasthenes to the court of the Indian emperor (Asoka's grandfather) at Pataliputra, the modern Patna (see W.E.P., 4 f.), and Megasthenes first describes the Ganges Valley to the Greeks.

[4] See W.P.O.B., 216, 243, 343.

[5] R.V., 5, 53–9, after G.H.V. The other rivers named here before Sindhu, namely Rasā, Kurmu, Anitabhā and Kubhā, are supposed to be tributaries of the Upper Indus, and Kubhā is supposed to be the Kophen or Cabul river, cp. G.H.V., 1, 522. In this latter location is a stone circle generally resembling the Keswick Circle on West-Mor-land border, and I have adduced a mass of evidence showing that these solar monuments were erected by Morites or Amorites. (W.P.O.B., 216 f.)

[6] R.V., 8, 20, 24.

Alexander), the modern Chenab, which appears to have probably joined the Ravi in ancient times near Harappa :

> " Maruta ! . . . bring us what balm soever Sindhu or Asikni hath,
> Or mountain or the seas contain." [1]

The Maruts were clothed " in robes of wool," [2] that is precisely as the Early Sumerians are clad in their contemporary sculptured representations and seals in Mesopotamia. And as confirming these Vedic records, we shall find that *more than one of those Indo-Sumerian seals from the Indus Valley are inscribed by " Maruta " (or Mer or Muru, i.e., Amorites).*

The Indus or Sindhu River was also an especial haunt of the " Horsemen of the Sun " (the *Aswin* of the Sanskrit, figured and named on the Catti coins of Early Britain) [3] and as a pair they called *Nāsatya* in Sanskrit, and *Nassāti* of the Khatti, Catti or Hittites ; and this pair is actually invoked in these seals. They were associates of the Maruts, and were the especial patrons of the Sun-worshipping Panch(-āla) or Phœnicians.[4] They are thus celebrated in the Vedas :

> " This river with his lucid flow attracts you
> More than all the other streams—
> Even Sindhu with his path of gold." [5]

Here " path of gold " appears to refer to the famous gold-dust of the Indus Valley sands referred to by Herodotus, Strubo, etc., see later ; and the Maruts are constantly celebrated in the Vedas as " the bestowers of gold to the Aryans."

The Indus River with its vast stretches of sandy desert plain and sparse population, was nevertheless the source of the modern name " India." The name, " India," arose through the Greek version of the corrupt Persian name of " Hindu " for the Sanskrit " *Sindhu*," [6] a name literally

[1] R.V., 8, 20, 25. [2] *Ib.*, 5, 52–9. [3] W.P.O.B., 58–9, 285–6.
[4] See previous note. [5] R.N., 8–26, 18.
[6] The famous Chinese Buddhist pilgrim and geographer, Hiuen Tsiang, in the seventh century A.D., records that the name " India was anciently called Shintu." B.H.T., 1–69.

meaning " The Ocean," with reference presumably to the wideness of its water in many of its reaches. The Greeks hellenized the Persian " Hindu " into " Indos," the Roman " Indus," whence our English " India."

The name " India " (or Sindhu) for the land now so called, or any part of it, is entirely unknown in the Vedas and Indian epics. That country is called from post-Vedic to modern times in Brahmanist literature " The Land of the B'arats " (*B'ārat-varsha*), a name synonymous with " *Barat-ana* " or " Land of the Barats," which I have proved to be the original form of the name " Brit-ain," [1] as given to Albion about 1100 B.C., by the western seafaring branch of the same Aryan Sumerian or Phœnician race of Barats, as the Eastern B'arats who civilized India of the Ganges Valley, and of the same Aryan Barat seafaring race as these " Sumerians " of the Indus Valley.

Why the ancient seaport of the Indus comes in modern times to lie so far inland, is to be explained by what is known regarding the rapid growth of the Indus delta, through the vast amount of silt and sand deposit brought down by that great river. The seaport of the Indus delta of Alexander's day, Patala, now lies some sixty miles inland owing to the modern advance of the delta.[2] The deposit brought down by the mighty Indus River into the Arabian Sea is probably much greater than that brought down into the Persian Gulf by the united Euphrates and Tigris rivers, the joint delta of which the latter is known to have extended southwards nearly 200 miles since about 3000 B.C., leaving the old famous Sumerian or Phœnician seaport of Lagash (or Sirlapur) nearly 200 miles inland, from the modern head of the Persian Gulf [3] (see map 2, p. 32).

Similarly, the present-day location of Mohenjo Daro so far inland as about 190 miles from the Arabian Sea coast

[1] W.P.O.B., 52, 65, 142, 168 f. [2] S.H.I., 101, and R.I., 129 f.
[3] See W.P.O.B., 263, etc. On delta formation in Orissa see my art. J.A.S.B.Proc., Dec. 1892.

may be thus accounted for. The precise position of Mohenjo Daro is unfortunately not shown even on the most recent maps of the Indian Trigonometrical Survey, unless it be "Mayhunjo Bohun" or "Mohana Dhora" in the south-east corner of the Larkhana district, and now on the island east of the main channel of the present-day Indus. But the official statement that the chief Mohenjo Daro foundations stand on the loop of islands with ancient remains in the Indus here—below the old site generally known as "Behker"[1]—fixes its situation sufficiently for the present. Having personally only passed along the Indus bank in this district and Harappa by the train some years ago, I have gathered the additional details in the following general account of these neighbourhoods and their topography from a study of the survey maps and from classic and other references.

Mohenjo Daro stands upon what seems to have been an early arm of the sea, in series with the still existing many-branched, land-locked arms of the sea extending over 300 miles inland in the Runn of Cutch, in the eastern portion of the vast Indus delta. Indeed, the second part of its name, *Daro*, appears to me to be the Indo-Persian *Darya* "the sea or water," a name which I have shown is derived from the Sumerian *Duru* "the sea or water," and disclosed to be the Sumerian source of the second part of the Aryan and Hittite god-name "In-*dara*" (the "Indra" of the Sanskrit), and of the Sanskrit *Dara* a "stream," the Greek *'Udōr*, and the Cymric *Dwr* "water."[2] Thus the name Mohenjo-Daro appears to have meant "Mohenjo-on-Sea." In strict series with this nomenclature we find that the Indus riparian district immediately adjoining Larkhana on the

[1] V.N., map, p. 67, etc. The latitude of Behker according to D'Anville is 27°12; but Mohana Dhora is 27°28 on the modern Indian Atlas Sheet No. 9.

[2] W.P.O.B., 323 f. On Sanskrit *Dara* or stream, cp. M.W.D., 470, which name is probably preserved in *Tari* "a boat" and *Tarsha* "ocean" (M.W.D., 439).

south is named " Lab-*Darya*," *i.e.*, " Lab-on-the-Sea." On the name Mohenjo, see later.

As evidencing the great depression in the basin of the Indus which still exists at Mohenjo Daro, we find that the Indus divides above that site into several branches, the outermost of which flowing twenty to thirty miles apart, unite again about eighty miles below and enclose several flat islands between their shifting channels. And significantly it is a point immediately above this depressed area of alluvium at the head of the old Indus delta, at Sukker, which has been selected for the building of the great barrage across the Indus, by which it is hoped this tract as well as the lower sterile delta will be converted into a rich oasis of cultivation, just as the Nile barrage has done for Lower Egypt.

It is on one of these large alluvial islands, at Mohenjo Daro, that the prehistoric buildings stand (surmounted by the later Buddhist monuments and monasteries of the Indo-Scythians), which have yielded these " Sumerian " seals, etc. Thus for several months of the year during the flood-season the river here doubtless still presents the appearance of a great inland sea, studded with islets, as oases in the sandy desert of the Lower Indus. But owing to the immense amount of sand deposited by the Indus, and the raising thereby of the level of its bed and of the delta, the tides are said to penetrate now no further inland than about sixty-five miles from the sea.

Significantly, this island location for the dwellings of the community who made and inscribed these seals, is precisely the position which was usually chosen for defensive purposes by the seafaring Phœnicians in selecting their trading-stations in a foreign country,[1] and such a trading-station and colony this evidently was, about 1400 miles distant from the

[1] W.P.O.B., 164, etc. Only latterly, after they had established firm relations with the natives, do the Phœnicians seem to have extended their buildings to the mainland.

old Sumerian or Phœnician seaport in the Persian Gulf (see sketch map 2). Moreover, it is significant to find, from the accounts of Alexander's historians, that in this neighbourhood were gold and silver mines, that is to say the very spot usually selected by the Early Phœnician mariners for their trading-stations near the coast.

The identity of the ancient name for this site at Mohenjo Daro with that found inscribed on the "Sumerian" seals unearthed there and at Harappa, is described in detail in a subsequent chapter (Chap. V.).

The Harappa site also, about 380 miles higher up the river and about 600 feet above sea-level, and the antiquity of which is attested, besides the seals, etc., by its great Buddhist monuments of King Asoka and the Indo-Scythians, stands on the left bank of the Ravi River, amidst a network of the dead channels of the Chenab, Bias and Sutlej tributaries of the Indus. The vast sea-like plain here is deeply scored by the dead channels of these ever-shifting great rivers which mostly arise in Tibet, like the main stream of the Indus itself. And along the banks of the Ravi and Sutlej to the great break in the Himalayan range, led and still lead the caravan-routes to the ancient gold-fields of Tibet, famous for their "gold-digging ants" of Herodotus and Strabo[1]—these ants, however, having a very matter of fact basis.[2] The relationship of Harappa to the dead channels of these old rivers is indicated in the survey-map. And it was doubtless an old confluence of two, if not three, of these old rivers that would be selected as an up-country trading-station by the early Sumerian or Phœnician merchants in their exploitation of the gold and turquoise industry of Tibet.

[1] H., 3, 98, 102–6. St. 15, 1, 44.

[2] The gold-digging "ants" (myrmeces) are described by Strabo as having "skins as large as leopards." They were evidently the large Tibetan rabbit-like marmots, which burrowed in the auriferous sand and brought gold to the surface. On my visit to the source of the Sutlej at the Māna-sarowar Lake at Mt. Kailas in Tibet in 1900, I observed how numerous were the marmots and their burrows on the plateau, some of the animals standing nearly two feet high.

The ancient buildings at those two sites erected by the people of the community which owned these "Sumerian" seals and now surmounted by later Buddhist buildings are briefly described in the preliminary report, above mentioned, which supplies the following amongst other particulars.

At each of these sites, we are informed "there is a vast expanse of artificial mounds evidently covering the remains of once flourishing cities, which to judge from the mass of accumulated debris rising as high as sixty feet above the level of the plain, must have been in existence for many hundreds of years. . . . At Mohenjo Daro the main street of the old city can still be discerned as a broad highway running from the south bank of the river toward the south-east, with houses fringing it on either side. What is surmised by the discoverer, Mr. Banerji, to have been the royal palace, stood at the point where the road emerged on to the quays of the river-side."

"Opposite to it, in the now dry bed of the river, are several islands from which rose the principal shrines of the city, the highest, and no doubt, the chief of them all being a massive Buddhist *stupa* raised on a high oblong platform, and surrounded by subsidiary shrines and monastic quarters." And it was under the foundations of these later Buddhist buildings on the islands where the seals were unearthed. "These (Buddhist) remains (at Mohenjo Daro) belong to about the second century A.D., when the Kushans were paramount in north-west India." [1]

The ancient buildings of the "Sumerians" at the island opposite the hamlet of Mohenjo Daro, lying below these later Buddhist buildings are thus described. "Deep down below the Buddhist monuments described above, or at other parts of the site appearing close to the surface itself, there are at least two other strata of buildings belonging to much earlier epochs and containing a variety of brick structures—

[1] M.R., 528.

the character and antiquity of which can only be surmised. Among these older structures one group is especially worthy of mention. Besides various halls and passages and chambers it includes a massive structure, apparently a shrine with walls seven or eight feet thick, pierced by several *conduits*. . . . In another part of the same group is what appears to be an altar of small *glazed* bricks, and provided with a drain of similar brickwork." [1]

At the Harappa site, " Mr. Daya Ram Sahni's excavations disclosed as many as seven or eight successive levels, demonstrating the long and continuous occupation of the site during many hundreds of years prior to third century B.C. (Stupa of Asoka). And throughout most, if not all, of this long period, burnt brick of a good quality was used for building purposes. . . . The smaller antiquities are generally identical in character with those from Mohenjo Daro. These smaller antiquities *from the two sites* comprise new varieties of potteries, both painted and plain, some fashioned by hand and some turned on the wheel, terra-cottas, toys, bangles of blue glass paste and shell, new types of coins or tokens, knives and cores of chert, dice and chess-men, a remarkable series of stone-rings, and most important of all, a number of engraved and inscribed seals—in an unknown pictographic script. Iron does not occur at all, except in the later deposits, and metal objects of any kind are scarce, particularly at Harappa." [2]

These seals with their Sumerian inscriptions we now describe and decipher in the next chapters.

[1] M.R., 528.
[2] *Ib.*, 528. For photographic illustrations of many of these objects and excavated buildings, see *Illustrated London News*, Sept. 20, 1924.

III

The Seals, their Stamp Shape and Animal "Symbols" and division into Official Signets and Grave-Amulets

THESE Indus Valley seals (see Figs. 1–3) significantly are not in the form of cylinders, or small rollers, such as were ordinarily used in Mesopotamia from the Sumerian period downwards for impressing signatures, by rolling upon, clay tablets. They are all, on the contrary, in the form of flat-faced, squarish or oblong signets for stamping with ink on parchment; and are thus stamp-seals, such as are found only occasionally in Early Mesopotamia and Susiana (now usually called "Elam") in the eastern arm of the Mesopotamian delta and its upland district, though more common in Cappadocia-Cilicia of the Hittites. This flat shape implies that the people using these seals were accustomed to write upon parchment and not upon clay tablets, as in Mesopotamia and Susiana. And parchment, as Herodotus tells us, was the immemorial writing medium of the Aryan *Getæ* or Scyths of Asia Minor, who I have proved to be the *Khatti*, *Xatti* or Hittites.[1]

Stamp-seals when found amongst the Sumerians of Mesopotamia are mostly circular or oval, though sometimes squarish or oblong like the Indus Valley seals. The latter shape is more frequent amongst the Hittites,[2] and also found to a less extent amongst the Susians, Cypriote

[1] W.P.O.B., 34 f.
[2] C.M.C., 150–163. H.H.S., pl. v., vii., ix., x.

Phœnicians and Kassis,[1] whom I have proved to be Aryan in race.[2] And, like the stamp-seals of the Sumerians, Hittites, Phœnicians and Kassi, these Indus Valley seals have a projecting knob on the back as a handle, which is usually pierced by a hole for suspension as pendant signets, or for use as amulets or charms and grave-amulets.[3]

The materials on which these seals are engraved are, we are told, "steatite, ivory, stone and paste."[4] They thus resemble those of the Sumerians, Hittites, etc. The engraving is executed in intaglio, with a technique much superior to and obviously of later date than, the archaic forms of the Sumerian word-signs inscribed thereon would lead one otherwise to suppose.

The seals are broadly of two classes, as we find by their inscriptions, namely, official and personal signets (of Aryan rulers or governors, ambassadors, ladies and priests), and grave or death-amulets of some of these and others of the same Aryan people. And significantly the inscription formulas on most of these amulets are couched in the identical form and words used in Hitto-Sumerian and Phœnician amulets, and as in the cup-marked inscriptions on the "prehistoric" tombs of Early Britain.[5]

The large bovine animals, the so-called "Bulls and Unicorns of the report"[6] figured prominently on most of these seals (see Figs. 1, 2, 3, etc.), we shall find are not employed as mere extra or religious or ornamental images, but as Sumerian pictographic *word-signs* with their Sumerian word-values, as component parts of the spelling of the place-names in the inscriptions.

The reason why the pictograph of the Ox came to be used in these seals as the basis of all the place-names recorded

[1] Stamp seals are also occasionally found amongst Assyrians and Medo-Persians, W.S.C., 2 f.; and amongst Susians (see later).

[2] W.P.O.B., 32 f., 47 f., 211 f., etc.

[3] *Ib.*, 238 f. In Egypt, in scaraboid form, the stamp seals are chiefly used as amulets—see Petrie on "Amulets."

[4] M.R., 528.

[5] See W.P.O.B., 237 f.

[6] M.R., 528.

therein, is now seen to be obviously because in this early stage of Aryan or " Sumerian " society, although the pastoral

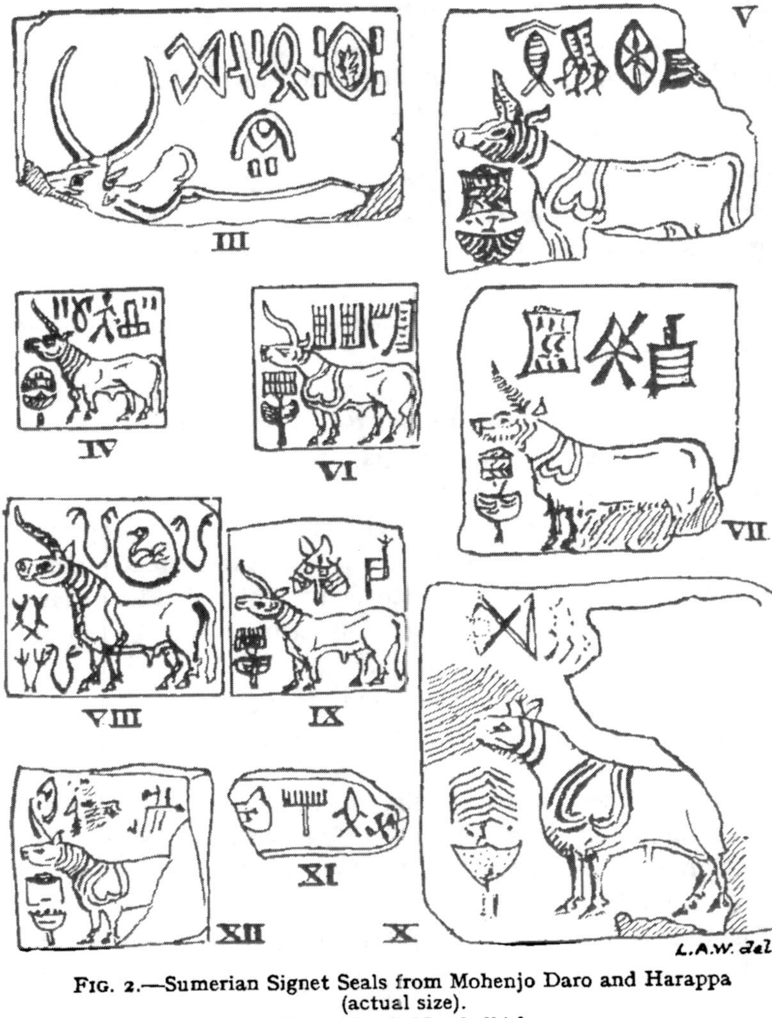

FIG. 2.—Sumerian Signet Seals from Mohenjo Daro and Harappa (actual size).
(After Sir J. Marshall.) [1]

stage had long been supplemented by the agricultural and industrial stage, cattle still formed the chief wealth of the

[1] M.R., 532.

Aryans in their settlements; and they continued to be the chief wealth of the Aryans, as we know, down to the classic Greek period, when the bartered price of valuable articles was expressed in terms of so many cattle.

The vast size of the herds of cattle at these Early Aryan settlements may be gathered from the statement of one

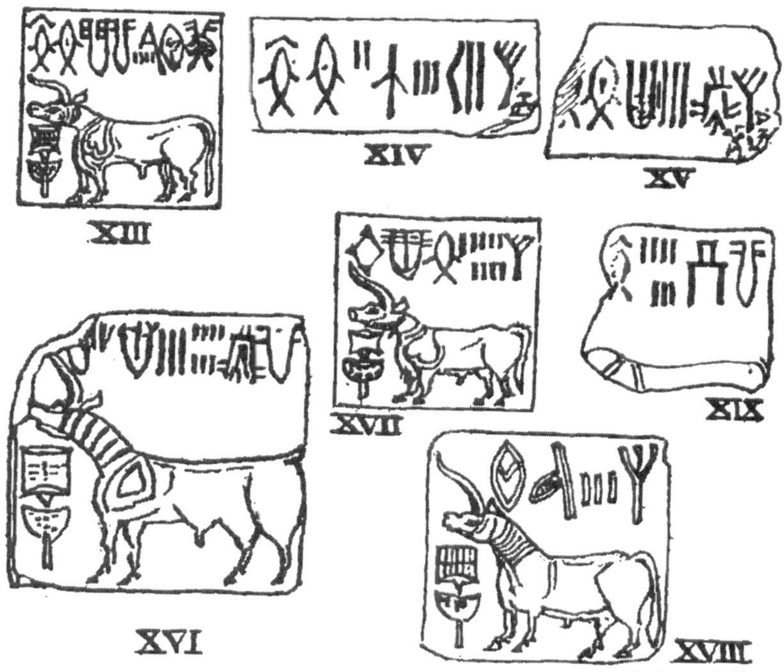

FIG. 3.—Grave or Death-Amulet Seals from Mohenjo Daro and Harappa (actual size).
(After Sir J. Marshall.) [1]

of the owners of these seals (No. I.), who boasts that he possessed "sixty thousand kine" in the Sindhu Valley (see later), thus far surpassing the herd in the stable of Augeias (3000), which has been deemed an exaggeration or fabulous.

Thus these Early Aryans or Sumerians at this period, about 3100 B.C. and later, appear to have regarded the idea

[1] M.R., 532.

of Cattle, with the addition of the word-sign for "land" or "fort," as the best ideogram to express the basis of their name for "town" or "settlement" or "dwelling." Hence the Sumerian name for "Ox" or "Cow," we shall find, also means "dwelling-place." This Sumerian word *Gu* or *Ga* for "Cow" on the seals, is now disclosed as the source of the Sanskrit *Go*, and of the English "*Cow*" and Scottish "*Coo*" and "*Kye*"; and as the source of the Sanskrit *Ga*, "abiding in," the old Indian Pali *Gā*(-mo) for "town," and it survives as the common modern Indo-Persian *Ga*(*n*)*w* "town" or "village," the Asia Minor *Koi*; and as *Gow* or *Cu* it was applied by the early Brito-Phœnicians as the suffix to their chief towns in Ancient Britain, *e.g.*, Cads-*cu*, Glas-*gow*, Linlith-*gow*, etc.[1] And this fact, now supported by these seals, offers important confirmation of the Sumero-Phœnician origin of the Britons.

The variety of cattle figured on these Indus Valley Sumerian seals are of great historical and economic interest, for this early period of about 3100 B.C. in regard to the early domestication of cattle. The cattle portrayed, and all of which face towards the right hand, *i.e.*, towards the West or sunset, comprise respectively the Water Buffalo (*Bos bubalis*), the humped "Indian" Bull (*Bos indicus*), and also probably the Goat or Deer-antelope—all of which are freely figured on Sumerian, Hitto-Phœnician and Kassi seals as sacred animals of the Aryan cultivators. The transverse bands on the neck of most of them appear to represent the necklet which sometimes adorns the sacred animal on Hitto-Sumerian, Elamite and Assyrian seals.[2]

The Water Buffalo here is especially interesting, not only from its being in those early days presumably indigenous to the lower Indus Valley, and possibly giving its name to the chief city, as we shall see; but also because its use on

[1] W.P.O.B., 78, 308.

[2] See W.P.O.B., 334, Fig. 59. For necklaced bull on Elam seals, see D.C.O.(L.)I.S., 468, 496; Assyrian D.C.O.(B.), 304.

these seals as a word-sign identifies for the first time the original form of a Sumerian diagrammatic word-sign of which the original hieroglyphic object represented has been unknown to Assyriologists.

That the animal in question is a Water Buffalo (see Figs. 1, 2, 3, etc.) is indicated not only by its heavy bovine form and wrinkled hide, but more especially by the crossed ribbing and wide curvature of its horns, the horns of all other bovines being smooth. The head is lifted higher than in the usual Buffalo habit; but this seems owing to the exigency of finding room underneath the head for the associated group of a bulky compound word-sign.

The Buffalo was well known to the Early Sumerians in Mesopotamia, and is figured in the seal of Sargon I. (about 2800 B.C.), and earlier; although modern zoologists believe that it is indigenous only to the Ganges and Brahmaputra Valleys and Indo-Malaya. It is represented by these writers to be unknown in a wild state in Western India, including the Indus Valley.[1] From its extensive representation, however, on these Sumerian seals, it would appear that in those early days it also had its home amid the rank, reedy growth of the water-logged, swampy banks of the Lower Indus. But in early seals the buffalo is figured as being tamed by the father of the king who founded the Indus colony (see Fig. 30, p. 22).

The humped Bull, commonly known as the "Indian" humped Bull or Zebu, appears to be figured on Seal No. III. (Fig. 2), as evidenced by the hump, with corresponding depression at its base, and the shape and curvature and smoothness of its horns. Although nowadays called "Indian," it is believed to be of Libyan or African origin,[2] and it was a sacred plough animal of the Sumerians and Kassis in Mesopotamia as attested by its representation on their sacred seals.[3] The

[1] B.M.I., 492. [2] *Ib.*, 484.

[3] See W.P.O.B., Fig. 12 (p. 49); D.C.O. ii., A. 26; in Elam, *ib.*, S. 199, 204; in Ancient Persian, *ib.*, A. 791.

animal figured on Seal No. XVI. (Fig. 3) is probably a Goat or Deer-antelope.

We now see more clearly than before how the Bull came to be regarded by the Early Sumerians or Aryans as sacred. Cattle forming the chief wealth, and yielding by their milk and butter a chief supply of food, and being as we find from the Early Sumerian seals the sole plough-animals, not to speak of their source of meat supply and the economic value of their hides and horns, the Bull as representing the herd came early to be considered sacred and associated with the Father-god Induru or Indara. Thus we find the latter even on the archaic Sumerian seals represented as wearing Bull's horns on his hat,[1] and pictured as attended by a Bull,[2] and in the Early Sumerian hymns Induru is called "The Bull of Heaven," just as Indra is called in the Vedic hymns. Similarly, too, Indara's archangel and his Sun when pictured in human form also wear Bull's horns on their hat; and his votaries or chosen people as "The Sons of Heaven" also are pictured therein as wearing these Bull's horns and at times Goat's horns, which latter Indara also wears sometimes. And this is the Sumerian origin, as I have shown, of the horned head-dress worn by our Aryan ancestors, the Goths, Ancient Britons and Anglo-Saxons.[3]

FIG. 30.—Gis'zax (Skt. Caxus), father of first Sumer king of Indus Valley, taming the Buffalo. From seal of Sibās'nı. (After Ward, 167.) Note he is duplicated for symmetry.

[1] W.P.O.B., Fig. 33, 239, Fig. 35, 245, etc., etc.
[2] *Ib.*, Fig. 39, 25, etc.
[3] *Ib.*, 239 f., 245, 250 f., 331 f.

IV

Sumerian Script on Seals: Its general Form and Peculiarities and its Language Aryan

The script engraved upon these seals, and supposed to be "unknown Indian picture-writing" and to have originated and "developed in the Indus Valley itself,"[1] was at the first glance clearly recognizable as Sumerian in type, and as containing many word-signs of the ordinary standard Early Sumerian linear hieroglyph script, as was current in Early Mesopotamia and in its adjoining province of Susa (or "Elam"). The remaining hieroglyphs, which vary somewhat from that Mesopotamian type, also proved, I found on examination, to be essentially of that type. They were somewhat more cursive in shape than standard Mesopotamian script, evidently owing to this script having been written by a people long accustomed to write with pen and ink on parchments, like the Earliest Sumerians, and unlike the later Sumerians in Mesopotamia, who substituted plastic clay-tablets (afterwards baked) for the perishable parchment, and wrote the hieroglyphs by a series of short dabs with a straight-edged style, for a pen with cursive writing tears the soft clay. Hence these seals preserve more largely the original curved lines of the archaic pictographic Sumerian, which are represented by a series of straight lines in the later standard Sumerian of Mesopotamia, and in its derivative, the cuneiform or "wedge-headed" script; and they are somewhat analogous to the curved "seal characters" of Ancient Chinese script.

[1] M.R., 548.

The general form of most of the script on these seals displays early forms of the Sumerian hieroglyphs, such as were current in Mesopotamia between about "4000" to 3000 B.C. and not later. Others of the signs on certain seals betray certain shortened conventional forms of the Sumerian script which only came into use at relatively fixed dates between about 2800 B.C., and 2400 and 2200 B.C. The palæographic inference thus dates the seals from before 3000 B.C. to about 2200 B.C.; and this inference is concretely confirmed by the personal names of fixed dates on the seals, as we shall see later on.

A feature of the writing is the not infrequent use of infixed signs in the interior of other signs, to show that the infixed sign is an integral part of that compound word. Another feature is the frequent attachment of the word-sign *As'*, which I have shown is the Sumerian origin of our English "*ace*" and Greek "*eis*," etc.[1] (and represented by I, the "*ace*" or "one"), to the end of a word-sign, and especially where it is used as the locative or "adverbial" suffix.[2] And already in Seal I., dating to about 3000 B.C., we have the vowel *u* almost in the form of a "ligature" and in Seal IV. it occurs as a ligature—the form in which it was regularly used later in Pali and in Sanskrit; and significantly it is written in the same *alphabetic* form which it possesses in these later Aryan languages and in the Greek and Roman alphabet.

Another important feature of this script is the systematic use of *short* parallel horizontal *strokes* to represent the "numeral" signs, as a sacred script, which in the Early Sumerian lithic writing of that archaic type were drilled as *circles*, forming shallow subconical depressions, the so-called "*Cup-marks*," which in the later clay-tablets were written as wedge-shaped crescents (*e.g.*, Fig. 5, col. 2, no. 6). This

[1] W.P.O.B., 240 f.
[2] Cp. L.S.G., 72.

fact is fully evident from the Death-Amulet series of these seals (Chap. VIII.), where the various series of these short horizontal strokes are especially numerous, and where they clearly represent the archaic circles and the later crescent wedges, and indeed cannot otherwise be explained or read. Thus the single short stroke is sometimes represented by a mere dot (in Seal XIV., Figs. 3 and 19, 3rd sign) which represents, the circle ; and the two short strokes represent not the word-sign *Tab* (or " two "), but the dual Sun (Day and "Night" Sun) word-sign, *S'amas'*, as "The Twin."[1] A vestige of the late use of such parallel semi-horizontal strokes for the circle or crescent signs is seen in inscriptions of Gudea about 2400 B.C. for the triad circle sign.[2] The obvious reason for this linear form of writing the archaic circles or crescents by short parallel strokes is the easier and more rapid writing when employing pen and ink on parchment, instead of the wedge-headed style on plastic clay. The practical importance of this observation is that in this linear form of writing the numeral archaic circle-signs, these word-signs (above one) are used with their mystic religious " *Cup-mark Script* " values of God-names, etc., as detailed and illustrated in my former work.[3]

Another outstanding feature of this seal script, and one to which I have already referred, is the use of the full pictorial figure of the Bull to represent its usual contracted form of word-sign of *Gu* or *Ga* for "dwelling" or "land," in place of the latterly used *Kur* and *Uru ;* and *Du* (or *Dun*), a " fort," is used for the later *Ki*, " land " (Greek *Gē*). But the use of the Bull sign in its contracted conventional form of the Bull's head was already in use about 3100 B.C. to designate this very place-name, as we shall see later on.

The *Language* of the inscriptions on these seals is standard Sumerian of the early agglutinative and condensed type,

[1] See Seal IV., Fig. 8, etc. This "Twin"=*Nāsatya* or Diosewir.
[2] B.W., 432, pl. 171 ; and Seal XIV., Fig. 19.
[3] W.P.O.B., 242 f.

with a minimum of grammatical expletives ; and it is, as I have proved in my previous work, radically Aryan and the language of the Primitive Aryans.

We are now in a position to commence the detailed decipherment of these seals.

FIG. 31.—Uruas' (Skt. Haryas'wa), first Sumer king of Indus Valley, and founder of First Phœnician Dynasty, with his five sons. From his votive limestone plaque at Tellsh about 3100 B.C. (After Heuzey *Déc.*)

Note in upper compartment the king with shaven head and face as a workman, carrying basket of bricks to build his Sun temple, with four sons and daughters in front (Mudgala holding fire-torch), and youngest son behind. In lower register king is seated holding cup (fire or libation). The names of the sons are graved on their woollen kilts.

V

First Series of Indo-Sumerian Hieroglyph Seals Nos. I. and II. from Harappa Deciphered and Translated

Disclosing owners as famous Vedic Aryan Fire-priests (Aus'ija *and* Kanwa) ; *and Harappa as a colony of* Edin, *tributary to Sumerian king* Uruas' (*"Ur-Ninā"*) *of Lagash ; and identity of Uruas' and his son "A-Madgal" with Vedic Aryan king* Haryas'wa *and* Mudgala *of First Panch(-āla) or Phœnician Dynasty about* 3100 B.C.

In commencing the decipherment of the hieroglyphs on the Indo-Sumerian seals, with the two which were previously found at Harappa before 1922 (see Fig. 1, i. and ii., p. 5), it will be noticed that their published photographs are in bas-relief, and thus represent *not* the seals themselves directly, but the stamped *impressions* of the seals in the orthographic or unreversed form of characters and direction in which the seals were intended to be read. On the other hand, all the published photographs of the other seals (Figs. 2 and 3) obviously represent the seals themselves, being in intaglio, and showing the bovine animals as well as the script facing in the reversed direction with reversed signs, as compared with the standard Sumerian in column 2 of the decipherment tables, and with the seal-impressions of these two Harappa seals.

As in Sumerian seals, the word-signs, although written in the archaic erect or perpendicular direction, in relation to the animals or other figures thereon engraved, are usually read with the seal turned on its left-hand side, I have therefore transcribed in column 1 of the following decipherment tables the hieroglyph script of the seals, with the latter lying on their left side.

In these decipherment tables, I have placed in column 2, alongside each of the seal hieroglyphs, the corresponding word-signs in standard Sumerian script (from Thureau-Dangin and Barton, T.D. and B.W. respectively) for comparison and to establish their identity, so that non-Assyriologists, for whom this work is written, may judge of the identity for themselves. And the Sumerian forms of the ligatured or infixed seal-signs are written separately. In column 3 is given the phonetic-syllabic value of each Sumerian word-sign. And below is appended my reading of the hieroglyph script—which is in the Sumerian language —with its literal translation into English.

The seal hieroglyphs, it will be seen, are for the most part identical or substantially so with the standard Sumerian signs, or with their early cuneiform shapes. When this identity is less obvious, the apparent differences are noticed in the notes.

In restoring the proper names on the seals by means of the Sumerian syllabic-phonetic values of their signs in roman alphabetic spelling, there is sometimes the usual uncertainty inherent in restoring Sumerian names, that owing to many of the Sumerian signs possessing more than one phonetic value (polyphony), the true restoration depends in such cases upon the true selection of the particular syllabic value. When there is more than one value I have usually noted them, and have selected that particular value which is in keeping with Vedic and Indian Epic forms of spelling proper names; for the Vedas and Indian Epics, as I have shown, supply us with the key, and *practically the only available authentic key, to the true restoration of Sumerian proper names.*[1]

SEAL NO. I. FROM HARAPPA.

Official Signet of AS'S'IAS' *the Barugu (Fire-priest) of Edin.*
The Vedic Fire-priest " AUS'IJA Kakshīvan," the
" *Bhrigu,*" about 3000 B.C.(?)

This seal (see Fig. 1, I., p. 5) is of immense historical importance, as in addition to establishing still more strikingly the historicity of the Aryan Vedas and Indian Epics as authentic sources of " Sumerian " history and the Sumerians as Aryans in race, it also recovers for us, for the first time, the actual original official seal (or seal-impression) of one of the most famous ancient Aryan Vedic Fire-priests (of about 3000 B.C.), who is the reputed author of several hymns in the Rig Veda—which hymns expressly locate him on the Sindhu or Indus River. In one of these Early Vedic hymns he is styled, as we shall see, " the far-famed *merchant* "; and he nearly always associates himself, and is associated, with the *Panch*(-āla), *i.e.*, the Phœnic-ians, and appears himself to have been a Phœnician. It moreover discloses the Sumerian origin and meaning of the Vedic Sanskrit name for " Fire-priest," namely, " *B'argu,*" " *B'argava* " or " *B'rigu.*"

The place-name " Edin " on this Indus Valley seal, a name which also occurs on most of the others of these seals, and a name for the Lower Indus city-port which survived there, as we shall see, down to the seventh century A.D., is of such critical historical importance and consequence that it demands our examination at the outset.

This name " Edin," with the identical ideograph monogram of the three conjoined word-signs as in this seal[2] (as

[1] W.P.O.B., 11 f.

[2] T.D., 428; B.W., 181.

in others of these seals) first seems to appear in the records of the famous Early Sumerian king, the so-called "Ur-Ninā" of Assyriologists, who lived about 3100 B.C., and had his capital at the seaport city of S'irlapur (or "Lagash," see map 2, p. 32) at the head of the Persian Gulf. The excavation of his old capital there by the French expedition of the Académie des Inscriptions et Belles Lettres, under M. de Sarzec, over a quarter of a century ago, yielded the rich treasures of his archives with a profusion of original official documents of himself and his descendants, great numbers of inscribed sculptures, seals, brick buildings, etc., which formed the chief foundation for the commencement of the study of Sumerian history and its high civilization.

"Ur-Ninā," who has hitherto been regarded by all Assyriologists as the earliest and greatest of known dynasts of the Early Sumerians, through the richness of his archaic monuments and those of his descendants, has nevertheless been summarily rejected recently along with his dynasty by Professors Langdon and Sayce merely because they could not find his name and those of his descendants in a late semi-fabulous king-list from Isin. But I find, on the contrary, that not only is "Ur-Ninā" with his descendants duly recorded in that Isin list, though unrecognised by these scholars, but his dynasty therein is made *the first of all the human dynasties of the Sumerians* (see App. IV.).

This Early Sumerian king was, I found, an Aryan Phœnician and the founder of the First Dynasty of the Phœnicians in Mesopotamia about 3100 B.C. His name, which has been arbitrarily restored by Assyriologists, without any clue to the original form of the name, as "*Ur-Ninā*,"[1] properly reads as I found by my new Sanskrit keys "*Uru-as'* the *Khād* (or Phœnician),"[2] and was substantially identical

[1] K.H.S., 65 f.; Cambridge Anc. Hist. Babylonia, I., 1924, 374 f.
[2] See Appendix I.

in name and relative position with the Aryan king "*Hary-as'wa*" of the Indian Epic King-lists, who founded the First Dynasty of the *Panch*-ālas or "Able *Panch*," whom I have proved to be the Early Phœnicians [1]; and Herodotus records the old Tyre tradition that the Phœnicians were located on the Persian Gulf before 2800 B.C. And his predecessors and successors, I found, bore substantially the

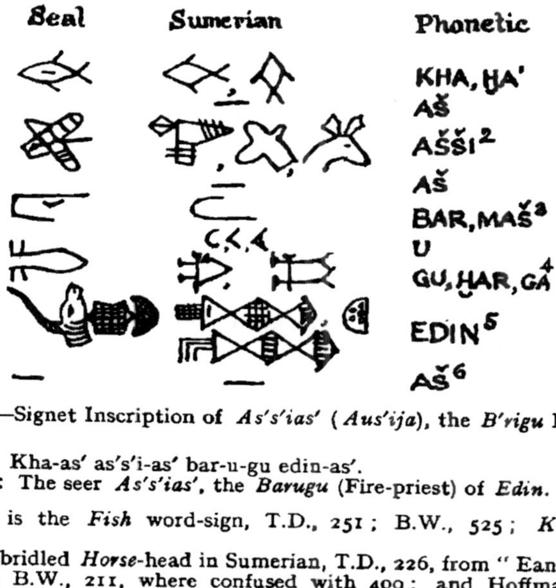

FIG. 4.—Signet Inscription of *As's'ias'* (*Aus'ija*), the *B'rigu* Fire-priest of Edin.

Reads: Kha-as' as's'i-as' bar-u-gu edin-as'.
Transl.: The seer *As's'ias'*, the *Barugu* (Fire-priest) of *Edin*.

1. This is the *Fish* word-sign, T.D., 251; B.W., 525; *Kha* value, B., 11817.
2. This bridled *Horse*-head in Sumerian, T.D., 226, from "Eannatum"; unbridled, B.W., 211, where confused with 400; and Hoffman tablet, W.P.O.B., 257, 412. For a more realistic figure of this Horse-head sign see Seal IX. On *As's'i* phonetic value, see W.P.O.B., 412.
3. Hook or Crook sign, B.W., 77a. *Bar* value, B., 1752.
4. Sumer sign Gudea, T.D., 74; El Amarna, B.W., 259. *Gu* or *'Har* "land," as well as "Ox" (M., 4038).
5. Sumer sign for Edin from Mudgala's seal, Fig. 5; lower from Gudea, B.W., 181, and cp. T.D., 427–8.
6. The *as'* here, and in the other seals, as a suffix to the place-name is clearly used as the adverbial suffix "at" (cp. L.S.G., 72); and not as meaning "the seal" (B., 15); or as "land" (M., 5).

same names and occupied the same relative positions in the Indian Epic lists of the Early Aryan kings as did his predecessors and successors on their own monumental records

[1] W.P.O.B., 12 f.

and in the King-lists of the Sumerians in Mesopotamia, though these Sumerian kings' names as "restored" in great part fictitiously by Assyriologists have hitherto masked more or less completely their identity, as we shall see.

As it is now discovered that it was this First Dynasty of Sumerian Phœnicians which first established the Sumerian colony in the Indus Valley, and its earlier members are referred to by name as Aryans in this connection, it is necessary to give here the list of the earlier members of this Phœnician dynasty as recorded respectively in the Indian Epics and in the contemporary inscriptions and King-lists of the Sumerians. And this comparative King-list strikingly shows how relatively faithfully the Indian Epics have preserved the original forms of the names of the Sumerian kings, as compared with the misleading names as conjecturally restored by Assyriologists.

First "PANCH(-āla)" or PHŒNICIAN Dynasty in Mesopotamia about 3100–2950 B.C.

Names in INDIAN EPIC LISTS *of Aryan Kings.*[1]	*Names in* SUMERIAN.	
	As revised by me.	*As read by Assyriologists.*[2]
1. Hary-as'wa or B'army-as'wa.	Uru-as' (the) Khād[3] or Bar-ama-'ha-as'	Ur-Ninā.
2. Mudgala, eldest s. of 1.	(A-)Mad-gal,[4] eldest s. of 1.	Akurgal, eldest s. of 1.
3. Pasenadi or Badhry-as'wa, s. of 2.	Bi(d)-as'-na-di, s. of 2.	Eannatum, s. of 2 (Entemena, s. of 3).
4. Divo-*Dāsa* or "Divine *Dāsa*," s. of 3.	En-e Tar-ṣi or "Divine Tarṣi."	En-li (Ene) Tarzi.

[1] Detailed proofs of these Indian Epic and Sumerian forms of these names in my *Aryan Origin of the Sumerians and Phœnicians.*

[2] *Cambridge Anc. Hist. Babylonia,* 1924, 374 f.

[3] See Appendix I.

[4] *A* in Sumerian="son" (B., 11328), and the prefixed *A* is the Sumerian intensive augment (cp. L.S.G., 95) just as in Aryan languages.

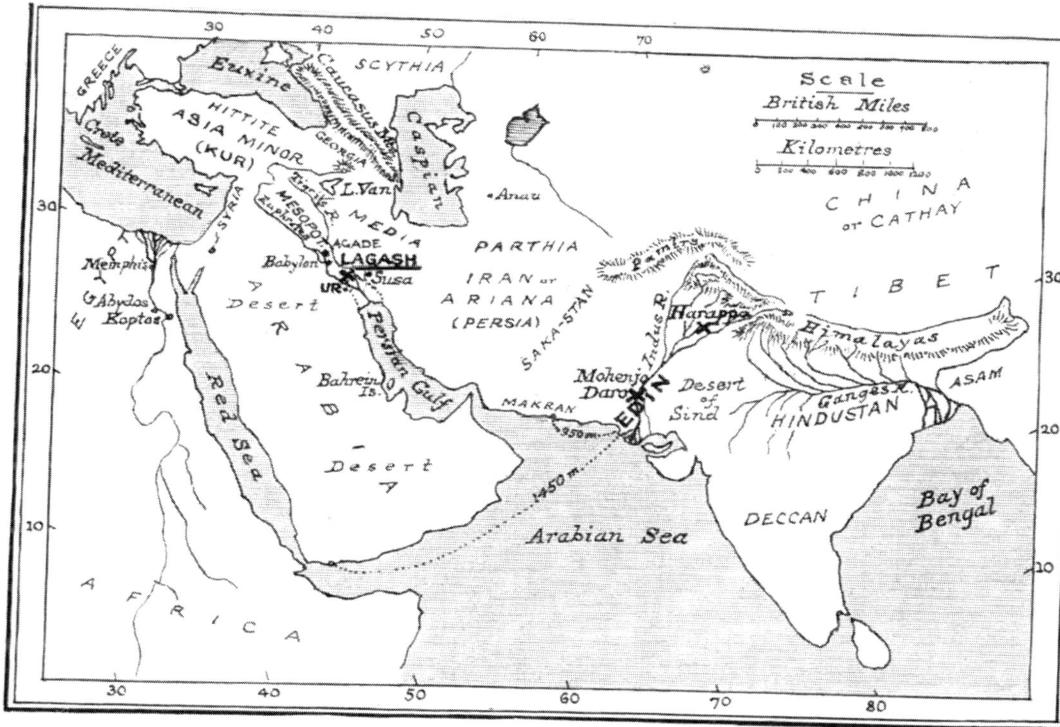

Map showing Relation of Indus Valley to Hindustan and Mesopotamia.

To face p. 32.

My revised forms for the names and the identities of this dynasty are also fully confirmed by the names and titles for them, which I have discovered in the recently found king-lists of Isin, as detailed in App. IV.

This first Sumero-Phœnician king Uruas' (" Ur-Ninā ") records on one of his documents that he " caused to be built two *Edins.*"[1] This now seems to denote, in view of our evidence which follows, his causing to be built the " Edin " of the Indus Valley, and the " Gu-*Edin* " sanctuary of the patron " Sun-god " of these Sumero-Phœnicians, which was situated in the plains of Lower Mesopotamia about thirty miles to the north of his capital on what seems to have been an old confluence of the Euphrates and Tigris, higher up the delta, and presumably a sacred site before the founding of " Lagash " or Sirlapur.[2] *Indeed positive confirmation of these two Edins of Uruas' seems forthcoming on Seal III.*, which appears to record that the owner of that seal-signet belonged to " The *Second* Edin " ; and one Uruas''s seal of the Indus Valley Edin (Fig. 5).

Although the name " Edin " came latterly to have also the meaning of " plain " and " desert," its ideogram consists of three conjoined word-signs, meaning respectively " dwelling-place or sanctuary " (*Ga* or *Gu*),[3] " Sun-god " (*Sir*)[4] and " earthwork or fort " (*Du* (?), *Dun* or *Din*). These three syllabic words thus forming its name, define it as " The Fort of the Shrine of the Sun-god," and this taken along with the statement that Uruas' caused it to be " *built,*" implies that it was originally a structure, and not a mere bare or cultivated " plain." And as a fact " Edin " is defined in the bilingual Sumero-Akkad glossaries as " The *city* of the

[1] Dec., pl. 2[ter], No. 2, col. 3, 7–8 ; translated, R.B., 62–3, where " caused to build." See Appendix II. for full translation. T.D. in his transliteration reads *a* for *min* " two," T.D., I., 12.

[2] It is usually supposed to be name of the district of Lagash.

[3] T.D., 417 ; B., 6113 (Sumerian *Ga* or *Gu*, B., 6103–4, Akkad *Kiṣṣu*) =" dwelling, shrine, sanctuary," M.D., 425.

[4] B., 1649 ; B.W., 72 ; and T.D., 15.

god Bel or Induru (*i.e.*, the Hittite Indara, and the Sanskrit Indra) ";[1] and it is referred to as "The *captured* land of Edin";[2] and also as "The *Saki* city (or land) of the Slave-girl (priestess),"[3] the meaning of which is found in her actual seals in the Indus Valley, Nos. IV. and XV. All this evidence implies that this "Edin" stood outside the principality of the Mesopotamian Lagash, and presumably outside Mesopotamia, in "The captured land" of the *S'aka* country of the Indian Epics ("*S'aka*-dwipa or S'aka continent")—a land famous for its Sun-worshipping *Maga* or "Magi," and which we shall find was traditionally located in the Indus Valley.

Now, an unique Early Sumerian "seal" was unearthed from the ruined buildings of Uruas'-the *Khād* (or Phœnician); and it not only belongs, I find, to this king's own reign, but also bears his own name, and gives details regarding his "minister" who governed Edin for him; and the name "Edin" is spelt therein by the identical compound ideogram as in these Indus Valley seals; and the script is in the standard Sumerian of the epoch of Uruas' of Lagash, see Frontispiece and Fig. 5.[4] Its great size and the fact that it is engraved orthographically and not intended for stamping shows it was not a seal, but a medallion of a victory, as we shall see.

This critically important "seal" (Fig. 5) has been discussed by various leading Assyriologists with varied conjectural readings of the names in its legend, in the absence of any key to the original form of the personal names to guide them in selecting the proper phonetic value from the polyphonous word-signs. The latest summary of these attempted translations and restoration of the names in this inscription is: "O Edin-mu-gi, minister of Gir (the god) who assists

[1] Cp. B., 4533. And on I.A. or E.A. as *In-duru*, see W.P.O.B., 13 f., 239, 244 f., 259 f., 315 f., 323 f.

[2] Edin-na sakh (or *lil*) *la*, B., 4532. [3] Cp. B., 4532, and Seal IV.

[4] Is engraved from clay tablet copy and not linear.

mothers in childbirth, Ur-Lugal-edina, the physician, is thy servant." [1]

On revising, however, the reading of the script on this seal, by my new Sanskrit keys to the form of the names of the

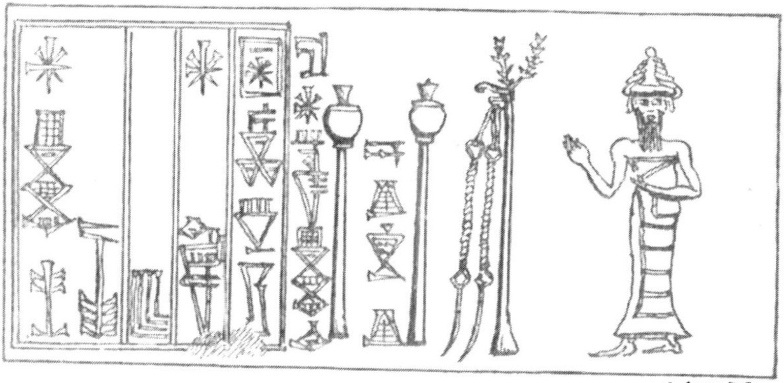

L.A.W. del.

FIG. 5.—Seal of *Mudgala*, Lord of Edin, minister of Lord *Ba'rama-has'a Uruas'*, King of Edin—the Vedic *B'army-as'wa Haryas'wa*—about 3100 B.C. from Sumerian seaport of Sirlapur on Persian Gulf.

(After Catalogue des Cylindres Orientaux, Musée du Louvre, Lib. Hachette, reduced ¾ diameter.)

Note his beard like the ancient Sumerians, and the ox horns on his hat, like the Goths and Ancient Britons, and see Frontispiece for photo.

Early Aryan Sumerian kings, I found that the inscription reads directly by other recognized phonetic values for these Sumerian word-signs :

As' edin mu-[2] gi [3] tax
As' bar [4]-ama-'ha [5]-s'a-ra
Uru-as' lugal-edin-na
A-zu us'-zu.

And this gives the literal translation of :

" The Lord of *Edin*, I the capturer, the minister,
Unto the Lord *Barama-'has'a* (or Lord Brahman-Seer)
Uruas', king of Edin—
The seer (or physician), thy servant."

[1] D.C.O.(L.), 1920, p. 10.
[2] M. 702=English "Me," and Sanskrit "*Mā*."
[3] *Ib.*, 1337. [4] B., 9179. [5] *Ib.*, 4032.

This Sumerian seal thus discloses that Uruas' (or "Ur-Ninā") of Lagash was "King of Edin" as well as Lagash, and that his "minister-servant" or governor "The Lord of Edin" and "The capturer," was as we shall see clearly his son, the crown prince Mudgala. And the long absence of the latter as governor of Edin in the Indus Valley would account for the paucity or absence of monuments of (A-)Madgal in Lagash and elsewhere in Mesopotamia.

The title herein of "*Barama-'has'a*" for King Uruas' of Lagash, strikingly and absolutely establishes his identity with the Aryan Panch(-āla) priest-king Haryas'-wa of the Vedas and Indian Epics, who bore therein the title of "*B'army-as'wa,*"[1] shortened in some of the Epics into *Bāhy-as'wa,* which is apparently the equivalent of the Vedic corrupt "*Bhujyu.*" This "Barama" we shall discover from next seal (II.) is the Sumerian source of the Sanskrit priestly title of "*Brahma*" or "*Brahman.*" And the additional "*'has'a*" (or *khās'*) is the Sumerian title of "Seer" (see next chapter), and *is the identical title of the seer in this Indus Valley seal, No. I.*, and it is held by the owners of several others of these seals. It is thus evident that this "Barama-'has'a" title of the priest-king Uruas', meaning "The Brahman seer," was latterly mistaken by the later Indian Brahmans as a proper name, and ignorant of its meaning they corrupted it into "B'army-as'wa" and "Bāhyas'wa." Thus the identity of the great Sumerian king "*Uruas'*-the-Khād and *Barama-'has'a* (or *-khas'a*)," with the Vedic and Epic Panch(-āla) or Phœnician king "*Haryas'wa B'army-as'wa*" is complete in regard to both his titles.[2]

The Sumerian title *As'* for "Lord" also, is significantly disclosed as the Sumerian origin of the Gothic title *Asa* or "Lord" for the early Gothic kings and princes in the Gothic

[1] B.D., 6, 46; 8, 12; Nirukta, 9, 23; cp. M.K.I., 2, 101. In Epics, W.V.P., 4, 144.

[2] W.V.P., 4, 144.

Eddas;[1] and is apparently the source of the Sanskrit *Isha* "lord."

The Sumerian word here for "minister," *Tax* or *Tāx*, is also of great historic and *British* interest, as it is the identical word-sign used for the Archangel minister or *messenger* of the Father-god of the Sumero-Phœnicians and Ancient Britons—*Tax, Das'i, Das'i* ("Nin-gir-su" of Assyriologists) and the *Tasc, Tascio* or *Dias* of the Ancient Briton coins and prehistoric cup-marked inscriptions in Britain.[2] This word *Tax* or *Tāx* is defined in the Sumero-Akkad glossaries with the divine prefix as "The Messenger or Minister of The Father-god Bel,"[3] which confirms the great mass of evidence cited in my previous work for the identity of the Sumerian *Tax* or *Dias'* with the Sanskrit *Daxa* or *Daksha* and the Briton *Tasc* or *Tascio*.[4]

The Sumerian word here also for "Seer or Physician," namely, *Azu* or *Uzu*, is disclosed as the Sumerian source of the modern Indian name "*Oja*" for a Medicine-man who practises Magic, and of Sanskrit *Oshadhi* or *Aushadhi*, "medicine," *Oja*, "granting strength," and *Ojas*, "strength"; and is probably the cognate of the Greek *Aug-e* and English "Augur."

The personal name of the owner of this seal is not given; but he is clearly the crown prince Mudgala or (A-)Madgal, as governor of his father's province of Edin. This identity is confirmed by his having the same title of "Lord" as the king (his father), and the further title of "Seer"; for Mudgala was an even more famous "seer" than his father Haryas'wa. Moreover, the objects represented on this seal were the especial emblems of Mudgala and *absolutely establish his identity*.

The objects figured on this Sumerian seal (Fig. 5), and to which Mudra-gi is pointing, *are diagnostic of Mudgala alone*,

[1] W.P.O.B., 240.
[2] *Ib.*, 243 f.
[3] B., 6165, 6171.
[4] W.P.O.B., 243 f., 261 f., 341 f., 447.

and are fully described in a Vedic hymn of Victory to Indra, which is ascribed to Mudgala himself.[1] This hymn and its early commentary represent Mudgala as owning vast herds of " well-pastured kine " (*gava* in Sanskrit, *i.e.*, the Sumerian *ga* or *gu*, " cow, ox, or buffalo ") to the number of " a hundred thousand," and he is called " Lord of Cattle." These cattle were raided by aborigines during his absence and only one bull was left behind. To overtake the raiders Mudgala harnessed this bull to his chariot, and yoked on the other side of the chariot-pole for balance (?) a stone-mace (*drughana*). His wife acted as charioteer, while Mudgala invoking Indra " touched " the beast *with the sacred stone-mace of Indra.* As a result the bull flew along so swiftly that Mudgala overtook the robbers and single-handed with his Indra-mace routed them and recovered his cattle. He is called in this hymn " Lord of Cattle " ; and significantly we shall see in the newly-found Isin king-lists (App. IV.) that Mudgala bears the title of " Protector of Oxen."

Now in this seal, with objects figured thereon which have hitherto been of unknown meaning to Assyriologists, Mudgala is seen pointing to the two stone-maces which worked this miracle ; and beside them is the chariot-pole from which depend the double-harness yokes, described in the Vedic hymn, as consisting of " thongs of leather," with their curved yoking-pins at their loose end.[2]

This complete identity of the names and relative positions on the King-lists of the owner of this Sumerian seal and his sovereign king of Lagash, with those of the Aryan *Punch*(-āla) or *Phœnician* Vedic and Epic crown prince and seer Mudgala or Mogalli and his father Barama-as'wa Haryas'wa, along with the literal description of the seal emblems therein, as preserved in his Vedic hymn, affords *one more striking*

[1] R.V., 10, 102.

[2] These pinned neck-yokes, wherein the yoke encircles the neck of the animal and the pin slips into the loop at the pole-end, are still used in India to the present day.

instance of the remarkable historicity of the Indian Vedas and Epics and their unique trustworthiness for the recovery of the proper form of the names in ancient Sumerian history, and as a key to the interpretation of the emblems on Sumerian seals and monuments which have hitherto been unknown.

Indeed, it now seems probable that the two large stone-maces, which have been unearthed at this "Edin" site in the Indus Valley, and figured in the official report,[1] and which are seen to be similar to the two figured on this seal, may be the actual pair of sacred stone-maces figured on this seal, which worked the miracle celebrated therein and in the Vedic hymn.

We thus find that the author of this Sumerian "seal" of about 3100–3050 B.C. was the Aryan Sumero-*Phœnician* crown prince Mudgala as governor for his father King Uruas' (or "Ur-Ninā") of Lagash of the remote "captured" province of the "Edin" of the Indus Valley. And that it was presumably graved by Prince Mudgala, or (A-)Madgal, as a votive offering to the temple of Induru at Lagash, to celebrate his victorious recovery of the stolen herds of kine, especially as the flower-pot sign on the carriage-pole, to which the Lord Mudgala is pointing, is the Sumerian word-sign *Mu*, "sing," as a song of victory, the actual words of which are preserved in our Vedic hymn. His own fine dignified portrait took the place of his personal name. And his title of "capturer" probably also denoted his annexation of the "Land of Edin" in the Indus Valley.

Resuming now the examination and decipherment of this early seal of "Edin," which along with Seal II. was unearthed at Harappa, as the names and titles therein require a separate chapter, we shall here proceed to the decipherment and translation of Seal II.

[1] B., 4347.

SEAL No. II. FROM HARAPPA.

Official Signet of Kan(-wa) the Barama.

The Vedic Fire-priest KANWA the "Brahma" or "Brahman," about 3000 B.C.

This seal also (see Fig. 1, II.) is of immense historical importance if, as appears certain, it recovers another of the actual original seals (or seal-impressions) of another related

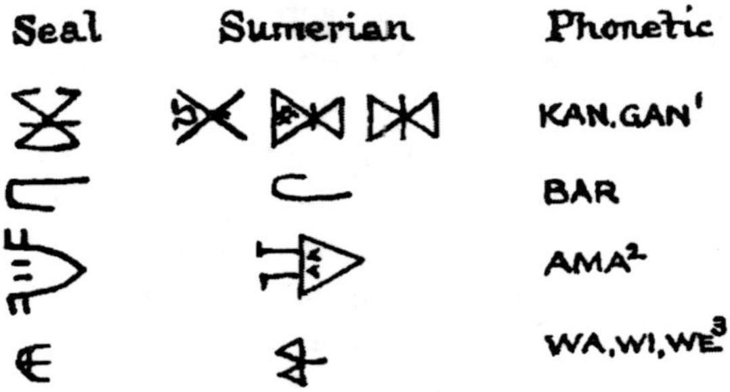

FIG. 6.—Signet Inscription of *Kanwa* the *Barama* or Brahman.

Reads : Kan(-wa) bar-ama wa.
Transl. : *Kan(-wa)* the *Barama* (or Brahman) the ear (of God).[1]

1. This seal-sign somewhat resembles the so-called "double-axe" sign, which, however, is closed at both ends and is of uncertain phonetic value ; but it is doubtfully placed by B.W., pl. 160, as a form of the *Gan* or *Kan* sign. Its middle stroke suggests resemblance to the *Elamu* or *Tum* sign of the period of Gudea (B.W., 387), but its recurved ends, which are also seen in next Seal II. and in XI., are against this identity. Altogether, except for its stroke, which may be the ligatured *As'*, it resembles essentially the *Gan* or *Kan* sign (see column 2), and cp. B.W., 160, which represents and means a "vessel" or "can" on a stand ; and I have read it as *Kan* (B., 4036). This reading seems all the more certain as it is followed by *wa*, which gives the Sanskrit form "Kan-wa," see foot-note 3.

2. This "Wild Bull" head sign *Ama* occurs in this form in documents of Manis'tusu, son of Sargon I. (B.W., 183).

3. The sign on the lower border of seal seems distinctly the *Ear* sign (see column 2) with value *Wa* or *Wi*, etc. (B., 7964).

group of famous ancient Aryan Vedic Fire-priests, called "*Kanwa*," the authors of many of the Vedic hymns, some of which are dedicated on the Sindhu River.[1] Kanwa the First and his "*Kānwa*" descendants associate themselves

[1] On the critical signs *Kan-wa*, see foot-notes to Fig. 6.

in their hymns with Panch-āla priest-kings, and are priests of the *Krivi*, *i.e.*, the Syrio-Phœnicians, and appear themselves also to have been Phœnicians. It also discloses the Sumerian origin of the Sanskrit name *Brahma* or *Brahman* for "a priest," and its hitherto unknown original meaning.

The identification of these personal names and titles on those two Indus Valley seals now requires a separate chapter.

FIG. 32.—King Bidas'nadi (Badhryas'wa), son of Mudgala and father of Divo Dāsa, with his captive enemies in "The Net of the Sun-god."

From his own victory Stele of the Vultures, about 3020 B.C. (After Heuzey *Déc.*)

Note he holds over the Net the Sun-Hawk or Phœnix, of which another figure is shown on a fragment of same monument on the left. For description of this Net and its survival in Brahmanism and Christianity see App. III.

VI

Personal Names and Titles of Owners of Seals I. and II.: The Vedic Fire-priests AUS'IJA Kakshīvan and KANWA

Disclosing also Sumerian origin of Vedic priest titles of " Bhrigu " and " Brahman."

The personal name of the owner of Seal I., namely, *As's'ias'* (see p. 31), appears to identify him conclusively with " *Aus'ija* " of the Vedas,[1] surnamed " Kakshīvan," who is called therein " the far-famed *merchant*," and singer " on the bank of the Sindhu," *i.e.*, the Indus. This identity is strikingly confirmed by the further discovery that the name of the Amorite lady in Seal No. IV is identical with that of the wife of this priest as preserved in the Vedas.

The reputed words of his hymns to Indra and his Fire- and Sun-horsemen, the As'win (the *Aesw* of the Briton coins), sung on the Indus about 5000 years ago, are still preserved in the books of the Rig Veda. Thus:

> " Bountiful Aswins, by whose aid the cloud shed sweet rain
> For the far-famed *merchant* Aus'ija—
> Wherewith ye helped Kakshīvān, singer of your praise.[2]
>
> " Aus'ija shall call for you The Thunderer (Indra) . . .
> *Sindhu*, giver of famous gifts, giver of fair fields,
> Listen with all your waters![3]
>
> " I celebrate these praises of Bhavya's son (my king),
> Dweller on the bank of Sindhu . . . I Kakshīvan."[4]

[1] Sanskritists have assumed that this name is a matronym, derived from *Usi'j*, a slave-girl, and meaning "son of *Us'ij*"; but it now seems, as we shall see, to have a different meaning.

[2] R.V., I, 112, 11; " merchant " is *vanij*.

[3] *Ib.*, I, 222, 5–6.

[4] *Ib.*, I, 126, 1–2.

"*Aus'ija*" was a name or title of more than one Fire-worshipping Aryan Vedic priest. It is applied as a patronym to the son of Kakshīvan in the Vedas. The Fire-priest Dīrgha-tamas, surnamed Gotama, a priest of King B'arata, and a reputed ancestor of Kakshīvan, who lived several generations before the rise of the Panch-āla dynasty about 3100 B.C., is also called "Aus'ija" in one of the Epics, and in post-Vedic literature, but its application to him appears due to a confusion by later Brahmans, as we shall see later on.

The "Aus'ija" of the Sindhu Valley, "the far-famed merchant" and Fire-priest, was a "Khattiyo" (or Kshattriya), *i.e.*, Khatti or Hittite and of the Kās'i clan. As a Vedic priest of Indra he is often called or calls himself merely "Aus'ija,"[1] but is identified with "Aus'ija Kakshīvan" of other hymns,[2] who also invoked Indra and his Fire and As'wins, and is the reputed author of several hymns of the Rig Veda,[3] and is called the son (or descendant) of Pajra.[4] Aus'ija Kakshīvan *resided on the Sindhu or Indus*, and he sings there the praises of the magnificent bounty he received from his patron "King Svanaya, son of Bhavya, dweller on the bank of the Sindhu, unconquered king."[5] This bounty comprised a hundred necklets (necklets were unearthed with several of the seals), ten chariots with "forty horses decked with pearly trappings, and sixty thousand kine."[6] He lived to the age of a hundred, and married in his old age the maid "*Wricaya*,"[7] *which name, or rather title, is actually preserved on the seal of the Amorite lady, Seal No. IV.* He had a son (or descendant) called Rijiswan, also bearing the patronym of Aus'ija,[8] and another son named Sukīrti.[9]

[1] R.V., 1, 112, 11; 1, 119, 9; 122, etc.
[2] *Ib.*, 1, 18, etc., etc.
[3] *Ib.*, 1, 116–121, etc.
[4] *Ib.*, 116, 7 f.
[5] *Ib.*, 1, 126, 1 f.
[6] *Ib.*, 1, 126, 2–4.
[7] *Ib.*, 1, 51, 13.
[8] *Ib.*, 10, 99, 11.
[9] M.K.I., 2, 452.

He is usually associated, and associates himself in his hymns, with King Haryas'wa B'army-as'wa (" Bhujyu ") and others of the famous Fire-worshipping kings of the Panch(-ālas),[1] thus presuming that he was a kinsman of the latter, as indeed his title of " merchant " at a river-port also suggests.

He has been confused by later commentators through his name Aus'ija with his ancestor Dīrgha-tamas, son of Ucathya, who in later Epics was also called " Aus'ija." And his name " Aus'ija " is supposed by Sanskritists to designate him as " Son of *Us'ij* the slave-girl," who was supposed to be the wife of Dīrgha-tamas, and the mother of Aus'ija Kakshīvan ; though this defeats the view that Dīrgha-tamas also bore that title (Aus'ija). *Fortunately the actual seal of " the slave-girl Us'ij " is found as Seal IV., from which we shall see that Us'ij was evidently the wife and not the mother of As's'ias' of this seal.*

Dīrgha-tamas, or " Tamas of the Deep " was, as we shall see, the grandfather of Uruas', and the " father " (or " forefather ") of Aus'ija Kakshīvan. He was a great sailor, and of the Kās'i clan of Khattiyos. Although he is not referred to as resident on the Indus, his seafaring is repeatedly referred to in the Vedas. Thus :

> " Dīrgha-tamā, Mamatā's[2] son, hath reached the tenth decade of life,
> He is the *Brahmā* of the Striving Waters, their charioteer (boatman) is he."[3]

His ancestorship of Kakshīvan is also implied in the " Gautama " title for the descendants of Kakshīvan—" Gotama " being a surname of Dīrgha-tamas, and latterly it was the famous family name of Buddha, the Sakya Muni, or " Seer of the Sakya tribe," who was presumably his remote descend-

[1] M.K.I., 1, 112 ; 116 ; 117, etc., etc.
[2] Mamatā, his mother, significantly was a priestess " of the race of *B'rigu* " (B.D., 4, 11).
[3] R.V., 1, 158, 6.

ant. His title as "Gautam Rishi" or Gautam-the-sage, is still common in the mouths of Hindus at the present day.

The priestly title of "*Barugu*," applied to Aus'ija Kakshīvan in the seal, now discloses for the first time the Sumerian source of the Vedic Sanskrit name for "Fire-priest," namely, *B'argu*, or *B'argava* or *B'rigu*. These Sanskrit variants of the same word denote a group of ancient Vedic Fire-priests who were skilled in producing the sacred Fire-offering by wood-friction, and they were largely Panch-ālas.[1] This Sumerian root *Bar*, literally meaning a "*Bar* (of Wood)," is defined variously as "Wood, Fire, Flame, Fire-god, Sun, priest or seer, exorciser, conjurer."[2] It thus explains its priestly meaning of "priest of the sacred Sun-Fire production from Wood." And "B'ar-tari" is still an Indian name for shrines of perpetual fire. The process of producing this sacred fire from the twin woods (*Bar*) is described and illustrated in my former work.[3]

His title of "*Khās'*" is the Sumerian for "Seer or necromancer,"[4] derived from *Khās'*, "a cut twig" or "cutting,"[5] presumably in the sense of twig-choosing by lot for divination. This title recurs on several of the other Indus Valley seals, XIII., XIV. and XVII.

Seal No. II. of "*Kan*(-*wa*) the *Barama*" (see p. 40) also recovers for us the actual signet seal of another of the great Aryan Vedic Fire-priests, and presumably also a Sumero-Phœnician. It also discloses the Sumerian origin of the priestly title of "Brahman."

Kanwa and his descendants called "Kānwa" are often named as priests and singers in the Rig Veda, and are credited with the authorship of the eighth book of that collection as well as with part of the first book. In those

[1] *E.g.*, Vadhry-aswa, Divodāsa, Cyavana, etc.
[2] M., 984; B., 1756, 1810; M., 998; B., 1802, 1841, 1844.
[3] W.P.O.B., 291–2 f.
[4] B., 4685–8. It has the infixed "Death" or "Fate" sign.
[5] *Ib.*, 368 f.

hymns the Kanwas invoke Indra, his Fire and Sun with his horsemen and the Maruts. Thus they sing :

"Praise nought besides, O friends; so shall no sorrow trouble you—
Praise only mighty Indra, when the mead is shed,
And say your praise repeatedly.[1]
Skilled in fair rites, with Soma (mead) pressed,
The Kanwas make light to Thee, O Fire!"[2]

Kanwa is celebrated along with Uruas' (B'ujyu) by Aus'ija Kakshīvan,[3] and thus must have preceded the latter. The Kanwas and Aus'ija's descendants were not rival priests, for Aus'ija and the Bhrigus are praised by Kanwas. Thus :

"The Bhrigus are like the Sun, like the Kanwas,
And have gained their heart's desire."[4]

So also the Kanwas repeatedly celebrate Uruas' (B'ujyu) and other Panch-āla priest-kings.[5]

"*Kan-wa*," we have seen,[6] is written with the signs of "vessel" (or "can") and "ear", and thus apparently meaning "Vessel of the Ear (of God)," a fitting title or name for a seer or diviner, or class of diviners.

Some at least of the Kanwas were priests of the Fire-worshipping Aryans on the Sindhu River. It is a Kanwa hymn which I cited on p. 8, invoking the Maruts (Amorites) to "guard Sindhu well and succour the *Krivi* in his need." And these Krivi or Syrio-Phœnicians are also the invokers in a Kanwa hymn to the Sun-horsemen.[7]

Kanwa the First, who was a *Khattiyo* and not a Brahman, is said in the Indian Epics to be the son of the B'arat king Aja-mīdha, an ancestor of the Panch-ālas.[8] Although the archaic form of his seal-characters is not out of keeping with so early a date, there seems no probability that the

[1] R.V., 8, 1, 1.
[2] *Ib.*, 1, 44, 8.
[3] *Ib.*, 1, 112, 5 f.
[4] *Ib.*, 8, 3, 16.
[5] *Ib.*, 8, 1, 15; 4, 23; 5, 22; 32, 171, etc.
[6] See foot-notes to Fig. 6.
[7] R.V., 8, 22, 12.
[8] W.V.P., 4–140.

Aryan kings mentioned in relation to Kanwa were on the Sindhu thus early. The Kanwa of this seal was more probably one of the later Kānwas. His title of *Barama*, or "Brahman," seems to identify him with a descendant of the "son" of Kanwa I., who, according to the Epics, was the first Kanwa "Brahman,"[1] though his father was a Kshattriya of the ruling warrior race.

The title *Bar-ama* now discloses the Sumerian source and meaning of the Sanskrit word *Brahma* or "*Brahman*" for priest. *Bar* = "Seer of the sacred Fire-producing Wood" (as above noted); and *ama* = "lord."[2] One of the earliest Vedic applications of this term seems to be to Dīrgha-tamas in the hymn above cited. But we have seen that it is used by the Phœnician King Uruas', the Haryas'wa of the Vedas and Epics, about 3100 B.C.

"Kan-we" or "Kan-me" significantly is also the name of the priest of the next seal to be deciphered, Seal No. III., of the new finds in next chapter.

FIG. 33.—Gis'zax (Caxus), son of Dīrgha-Tamas, and father of Uruas' (Haryas'wa) watering the Buffaloes after taming them.
From seal of Sargon I., about 2800 B.C., in De Clercq collection.
Note his leonine head, and duplication for symmetry.

[1] W.V.P., 130, 140. Medhatithi, "descendant" or "son" of Kanwa. And cp. P.I., 225 f.

[2] B., 4543. In Akkadian *Bārū* = "seer, diviner, magician," and is interpreted as "the one who *sees*, *beholds* or *discerns*." Cp. M.D., 183.

VII

OFFICIAL SIGNET INDO-SUMERIAN SEALS FROM MOHENJO-DARO AND HARAPPA DECIPHERED AND TRANSLATED

Disclosing Signets of KAN-WE ; *of Slave-girl Sun-priestess* USIZ *of* URIKI (*Vedic " Us'ij-Wricayā," wife of owner of Seal I.*) ; S'US'ENA *of* GUS'A (*S'usin of Ur and Indian " Sushena "*), TAX *minister of* SAGUNU *of* AGDU (*Indian " Daxa " re S'akuni of Ayodhya as Sargon of Agade*) ; SAGARA *as Sargon I.* ; DAMU *the* GUTI *or Goth, etc., etc.* ; *and Indian Epic versions of* SARGON I., GUDEA, DUNGI, BUR SIN I. *and* S'U SIN *of Ur Dynasty.*

THE seals now deciphered in this chapter represent the *Official Signet* Seals of the recently-found collections from the excavations at Mohenjo-Daro and Harappa in the Indus Valley—the Grave-Amulets of these finds, forming a separate series, are relegated to the next chapter. As no information is given in the official report as to which of the two sites yielded the particular seals, the special site of each individual seal cannot be stated at present.

The photographs of this second series of seals are direct photographs of the seals themselves, and thus show the hieroglyphs in the reverse form and direction from what they would be in the seal-impression, in which they were intended to be read. In our reading of these hieroglyphs, therefore, it is necessary to turn the seal on its *right* side, when the hieroglyphs will appear in their due sequence, *but in reversed form*, as will be seen by comparison with their standard Sumerian equivalent signs in column 2 of the decipherment tables. And in this reversed way, as on the seals, I have accordingly transcribed these seal hieroglyphs in the following decipherment tables.

SEAL NO. III.

Official Signet of KAN(-WE) *priest of Khaitisig at E(din).*

This seal (see Fig. 2, III.), the lower part of which with the name of the city is wanting, is the signet of a "Kanwa" priest, who presumably was a different individual of that group of priests from the holder of Seal No. II., in view

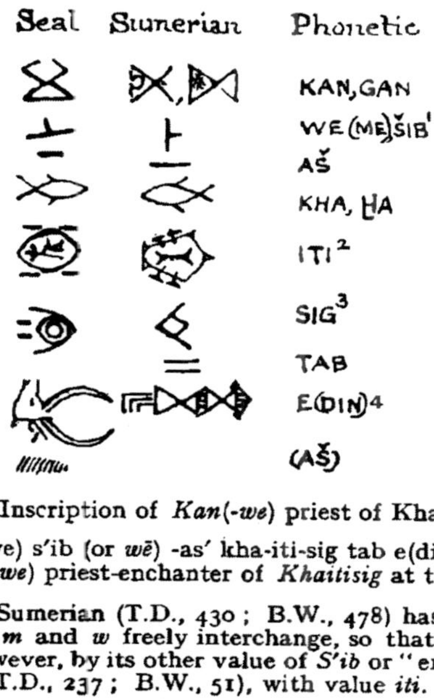

FIG. 7.—Signet Inscription of *Kan(-we)* priest of Khaitisig at E(din).

Reads: Kan(-we) s'ib (or *wē*) -as' kha-iti-sig tab e(din-as').
Transl.: *Kan(-we)* priest-enchanter of *Khaitisig* at the second e(din).

1. This sign in Sumerian (T.D., 430; B.W., 478) has ordinary phonetic value of *me*, but *m* and *w* freely interchange, so that it might read *we*. I have read it, however, by its other value of *S'ib* or "enchanter," see text.
2. Sumer sign (T.D., 237; B.W., 51), with value *iti*.
3. T.D., 256.
4. This Bull on seal is not a buffalo, and therefore not the usual first part of the compound "Edin" sign; but is the *Gu* or *'Har* sign (T.D., 74; B.W., 259); yet we have found in Fig. 4 that the unbarred horns are also used in the Edin sign, column 2, lower sign.

of the different variety of hieroglyph used for the first sign, and the absence of the title " Barama."

The personal name here, as also in Seal II., is *Kan*—the *wa* affix of the Sanskrit form of the name " Kanwa " we have seen was not directly attached to the name in Seal II.; and although the second word-sign in this seal might possibly read *we*, and thus give the name as " Kan-we," I have preferred the more usual Sumerian value *S'ib*, " enchanter," which I have shown is the Sumerian origin of our English "Sibyl."[1]

" *Khaitisig* " appears to be the name of the city of Lower Edin, as we shall see in Chap. X. on the Place-names. It is possible, however, that this name represents the official title of " high-priest," which is usually written " *Khattesig* " in Sumerian, though rendered by Assyriologists " Patesi."

The sign following " Khaitisig," consisting of two short horizontal lines, may read either " two " or " second," or " the Sun "; [2] and it may be attached either to Khaitisig or to the next following word " Edin " (?). It thus may designate this Indus Valley Edin as " the second Edin," and we have seen that King Uruas' built " two Edins."

" Edin " is probably the name of the shrine, fort, or city-state name here, where the rest of the word-sign of this compound place-name is broken off and wanting. For although the bull here is not a buffalo, which with its cross-barred horns usually form the first part of the name " Edin," we have seen in Fig. 4 (second column) that unbarred horns also designate " Edin " in this compound monogram sign.

SEAL NO. IV.

Official Signet of US'IZ, *the Slave-girl of the Sun, at* URIKI.
The Vedic US'IJ or WRICAYĀ, wife of Aus'ija (of Seal I.).

This critically important small seal (Fig. 2. IV.) conclusively corroborates and complements the seal of Aus'ija

[1] W.P.O.B., 243, 248.

[2] See foot-note 5 to Fig. 8.

the B'rigu or Fire-priest of Edin (Seal I.), whilst further confirming the historicity of the Vedas and Indian Epics.

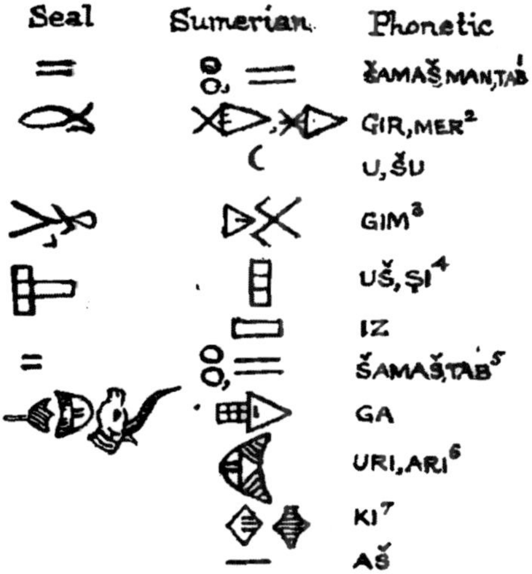

FIG. 8.—Signet Inscription of *Us'iz*, the slave-girl of the Sun at *Uriki*.

Reads : Tab mer-u gim us'-iz s'amas' uri-ki-as'.
Transl. : The Sister Meru, the Slave-girl *Us'iz* of the Sun(-shrine) at *Uriki*.

1. This word-sign ordinarily reads in the linear script *Tab* (B.W., 144), literally " two " (and thus the source of the English " two," Scots " twa," Skt. *dwa* or *dva*) and " second," and secondarily " brother or sister " (M., 2449). But in the sacred " numeral " script, it means " the Sun," see foot-note 5.

2. This seal-sign seems a compound of the Spear sign (col. 2., T.D., 4 ; B.W., 10, pl. 192) ; with the value *Gir* (B. 300) or *Mer* (B., 301), and the attached sign of *S'u* (B., 8644) or *U* (B., 8645). It thus may read either *Gir-s'u* or *Mer-u*.

3. The Sumer sign in col. 2 is from Manis'tusu (B.W., 501), with value *Gim*, " slave-girl " (B., 11135).

4. This sign is not *Nin* (T.D., 335 ; B.W., 499), but a compound of *Us'* (T.D., 469 ; B.W., 481) and *Iz* (T.D., 402 ; B.W., 258) ; and cp. B., 5698 on value *Iz*.

5. This pair of two short strokes may = *tab*, " two," with meaning as in foot-note 1. But from a study of the " numeral " script in this and others of these seals, we shall find that in the Amulet series this linear " numeral " script represents the archaic circles and crescents, with their religious values. Hence this sign = " The Sun as *S'amas'* or *Buzur* or *Man* (B., 9960, 9944, etc.) ; and here it seems to mean " of the Sun (-shrine)."

6. This seal-sign is clearly *Uri* (B.W., 316, pl. 83) with value *Uri* (B., 7308) and in Assyrian " *Akkadu*." It has also value of *Ari*, *i.e.*, " Arya or Aryan," and is an epithet of Amorites (M., 5328 ; B.W., 316) and Ur city.

7. The sign is clearly *Ki* (T.D., 254 ; B.W., 419).

The personal name of " *Us'iz*, the Slave-girl at Uriki " on this seal is certain and unequivocal. The prefixed title, however, in the word-signs 1–3 and the word-sign following the name *Us'iz* (no. 7, see Fig. 8, column 2) being polyphonous, may be read variously. These (1–3) may read either " The Sister (or companion) of Girs'u "—Girs'u being the suburb of the capital of King Uruas' at Sirlapur, containing the great Sun-temple there—or this group may read " The Mer-u (or ' Amorite ') Sister " ; whilst the seventh sign may read either " sister " or " second " or " Sun (-shrine)." If the reading is " second," it would imply that there had been a previous holder of the name " Us'iz." But be this as it may regarding the prefixed and affixed titles, it in no way affects the certainty of the reading of the personal name and place-name of " Us'iz, the Slave-girl at Uriki."

The name " *Us'iz*, the Slave-girl at Uriki " clearly discovers the Sumerian original of the Vedic name " *Us'ij* " for the traditional " slave-girl " wife of the Vedic and Epic seer Aus'ija Dīrgha-tamas. On the other hand, her country name of *Uriki* is clearly the Sumerian original of the Vedic " *Wricayā* " (or " of Wrica "), the Vedic name for the wife of Aus'ija Kakshīvan (Seal I.), the " son " or " descendant " of Dīrgha-tamas. Thus in a battle-hymn to Indra, celebrating the achievements amongst others of Aus'ija Kakshīvan's son Rijiswan, the mother of the latter is named *Wricayā* :

> " To old Kakshīvan, the mead-presser, skilled in song,
> O Indra, thou didst give the youthful *Wricayā*." [1]

" Us'iz " of this seal, a name which so literally equates with Vedic and Indian Epic " Us'ij, the Slave-girl," means in Sumerian " The Message-giving enchantress " (*Us'*),[2]

[1] R.V., 1, 51, 13.
[2] This *Us'* is defined in the glossaries (B., 10557) as=Akkadian *temu*, " message decision edict," cognate with *tamū* " incantation " and *tammaú*, enchanter (cp., M.D., 356, 1167).

plus " Wood " (*Iz*,[1] for divination ?). It was thus a fitting name or title for an augur or oracular Sun-priestess of the Edin temple of Dāsi or Dias' (" Nin-gir-s'u ") the Sumero-Phœnician Sun archangel of Induru (or Indra) their One Father-god, and the " Dias " or " Tascio " of the Barat Phœnicians on the Ancient Briton coins.[2] And she is actually styled on her seal " Slave-girl of the Sun." And Edin was called by the Sumerians, as we have seen, " The *Saki* city (or land) of the Slave-girl," wherein *Saki* is as seen later the S'āka (or Sacæ or Goth) Land of the Indus Valley ; and it was also called by the Sumerians " The city (or land) of the Priest-queen of Bel." [3]

If " Us'ij " was really the wife of Aus'ija Dīrgha-tamas and the mother of Aus'ija Kakshīvan, and not the wife of the latter, as the later post-Vedic legend alleges ; and so gave to Kakshīvan his title of " Aus'ija " as a matronym, meaning " Son of Us'ij," then she must have occupied a higher position than the " father " Dīrgha-tamas, great seer though he was, and this would be explained by her being the augur " slave " of Das'i or " Nin-gir-s'u " at the Sun temple in Edin.

It is therefore necessary here to relate this post-Vedic legend that she was " the slave-girl " wife of Dīrgha-tamas and the mother of Kakshīvan. This legend states that Dīrgha-tamas, a contemporary of King B'arata, if not his son,[4] was the son of the Fire-priest Ucathya (or in other Epics the son of King Kās'i),[5] and was expelled from S'arad-want through a quarrel with his younger brother, and set adrift down " the river," and was stranded in the Anga country. There he was given by the king of that country a slave-girl (*dāsi*) from the royal household, by whom he had

[1] B.W., 258. [2] W.P.O.B., 338 f.

[3] B., 4532, wherein the word-sign *Silag* has the ideograph values of " Woman " + " priest-queen " (B., 3385), also Bel (B., 3378).

[4] His brother was the " son " of King Bharata, W.V.P., 4, 134.

[5] *Ib.*, 4. 32.

as son, the seer Aus'ija Kakshīvan, from whose title *Aus'ija*, it is assumed by early Vedic commentators that his mother's name was "*Us'ij*."[1]

This slave-girl's name or title, however, in the Mahā-B'ārata is Aus'inarā, *i.e.*, "of Us'inara."[2] Now the Us'inaras were a clan or tribe of S'aka people, who included the S'ibi or Sivi tribe, usually identified with the "*Sib*-oi" tribe found by Alexander in the Upper Indus Valley at the junction of the Ravi and Chenab, not many miles from Harappa, and Alexander sold many of the captured Siboi as slaves. Moreover, the early rulers of the Us'inaras, according to the Epics, were descended from S'rinjaya, who was a Panch-āla and founded a dynasty called after his name.[3] As "Amorite" was a title of the sea-going Panch-ālas or Phœnicians,[4] "the Amorite slave-girl Us'iz" may have been an Amorite princess prisoner of war captured by the king of Anga and enslaved as Alexander did with the Siboi, and restored to the Sumerian Amorite colonists at Edin—though this Anga is not to be confused with the later "Anga" name transplanted by later Indian Brahmans to a district on the Ganges. By another account Dīrgha-tamas himself was the father of the Anga kings.[5] But the title of "slave-girl" was, we shall see later, "slave or servant vestal virgin of the Sun-temple."

On the whole, therefore, it would appear probable that "the slave-girl of the Sun, *Us'iz*," of this seal, who bears also the title of "*Uriki*," and thus equating with "*Wricayā*," who was the wife of Aus'ija Kakshīvan, was really the wife of the latter, whose proper Sumerian name as found on Seal I. was *As's'ias'*, the source of the Sanskrit *Aus'ija*. And that the later Brahmans, from the similarity of the name *As's'ias'* to *Us'ij* the slave-girl, confused the two names, and invented the legend of the marriage of Us'ij

1 B.D., 4, 21–25.
2 M.B., 2, 20, 802.
3 W.V.P., 4, 120, 144.
4 W.P.O.B., 216 f.
5 W.V.P., 4, 122.

to Dīrgha-tamas in order to explain the name "Aus'ija" as a matronym of "Us'ij."

On "Uri-ki" as "The city of the Amorites," see Chap. IX. on the Place-names.

The actual Grave-Amulet of this "Slave-girl priestess of the Sun" appears to be found in Seal XV., implying that her tomb in Edin of the Indus Valley has been exhumed in the excavations there.

The Death-Amulet "seal" of another Amorite Sun-priestess called "Nina" from Smyrna, and written in archaic Sumerian script of this or a still earlier period, has been figured, deciphered and translated by me in my former work.[1] And significantly she is designated therein by *the identical sign of "Uri" or "Ari" for "Amorite," as in this seal.*

SEAL NO. V.

Official Signet of Prince S'US'ENA *of Edin (or Agdu? or S'aki), later King* S'U-SIN *of the* UR *Dynasty of Mesopotamia*

The Indian Epic SUSHENA the *Kus'i-ka,* "brother" of Paras'u-Rama and great-grandson of King GÁDHI, the Sumerian GUDIA ("Gudea"), about 2350 B.C.

This seal (Fig. 2, V.), with its associated new evidence from the Indian Epics, is of first-class historical importance for reconstructing several lost chapters in the history of the Sumerians; and confirms still more strikingly the remarkable historicity of the Indian Epics as authentic sources of new Sumerian history hitherto unknown to Assyriologists.

It discloses, along with its associated Indian Epic tradition, *important new history regarding the hitherto unknown*

[1] W.P.O.B., 257–8; 413–14.

origin of "Gudea's Dynasty," and the rise of the so-called "Third Dynasty of Ur," which links up many isolated facts in Sumerian monumental history of that period hitherto more or less unaccountable. It discloses the proper form of the names of the members of those two dynasties which have hitherto been "restored" conjecturally, mostly in false forms, from polyphonous word-signs, through want of a key to the proper forms of the names which the Indian Epics now supply. And it discloses the crown prince and successor of "Bur Sin I." of the Ur Dynasty, like the son and heir of the Sumero-Phœnician Uruas' or "Ur-Ninā" long before him, as governor of the tributary state of Edin in the Indus Valley about 2350 B.C.

There were four different princes or kings named "*Sushena*," who are mentioned in the Indian Epics. Firstly, is Sushena of the *Kus'a* dynasty, a maternal great-grandson of King *Gādhi*, who I found was the famous Sumerian emperor generally called "*Gudea*," but now seen to be properly "Gud*i*a." [1] Two others who seem rather legendary were the sons respectively of the man-god Krishna and his father Vasudeva; [2] and a fourth was a son of Parixit, a descendant of Kuru.[3] This seal is seen to be the signet of the first named; and he proves to be identical with *S'u-sin, S'u-as'-sin, or Su-as'-en-zu* the historical king of the "Ur Dynasty," hitherto called "Gimil Sin," who reigned about 2350 B.C. and presumably identical with *S'u-s'e-en* . . . who is mentioned in a stele of King Silhak of Sus'a (Elam) who reigned about or shortly after that same epoch [4]—Sus'a having been tributary to the Sumerian dynasties of Ur, etc.

This *S'us'ēna* of this seal is now seen to be the Sushena of the *Uru* branch of the "*Kus'a*" Dynasty of the Indian Epics, the ancestry and members of which are recorded therein as in the following genealogical table. From this

[1] The second syllabic sign in "Gu-de-a" has also the phonetic value of *di* (cp. B., 6715.)

[2] W.V.P., 5, 78; 4, 110.

[3] M.B., I., c. 94.

[4] S.T., V., x–xi.

table it will be seen that the "Ur Dynasty" of Dungi branched off from the Kus'a main line with the marriage of Gudia's daughter to "*Uru-Ricika,*" a B'rigu Fire-priest,

FIG. 9.—Signet Inscription of *S'us'ēna* prince of *Edin* (or *Ag-du ?* or *S'aki ?*) Land.

Reads: S'u-s'e-en-'a sag gū edin (or *ag-du* or S'a-ki)-as.
Transl.: *S'us'ēna* prince of *Edin* (or Ag-*du* or S'aki ?).

1. On this Wheat-ear sign, cp. B.W., 323 and 175, and pl. 43 and T.D., 519, Appendix. On its *S'e* value, B., 7433, 4403.

2. T.D., 209; B.W., 354. Its value *'A* (B., 8285) and *Umun* or *S'umun*, "prince or lord" (B., 8284 and 9478). This *S'umun* appears to be Sumerian origin of Sanskrit *S'wamin* "a lord."

3. This broken sign seems clearly T.D., 176; B.W., 291, *i.e. Zag* or *Sag* "prince" *not* "king" (B., 6468.) It is not T.D., 175, as it has two transverse bands and is not reversed.

4. *Gu* or *Ga* as in Seal IV., "shrine or dwelling," but here presumably part of proper name.

5. This sign is clearly *S'A* or *AG* sign (T.D., 52; B., 2774). The vertical median stroke first appears in Gudea period (B.W., 110).

6. T.D., 235; B.W., 417, with value *Du*. It might also be *Ki*, "land or city." T.D., 254; B.W., 419.

who established a new dynasty, and who is seen by the next table to be identical with the founder of the "Ur Dynasty," namely, "*Uru-as'-zikum,*" hitherto read as "Ur Nammu" or "Ur Engur," and the father of "Dungi" or *S'amu-Dukgin* —the "*Jama-Dagni*" of the Indian Epics. The Kus'a line of kingship ended with this marriage of Gudia's daughter to Uru, as Gudia's son Vis'wā-Mitra became a devoted Sun-priest; and the use by *S'us'ēna* of the title "Gus'a" on his seal (if it be there), appears to be in a territorial sense.

Genealogy of "Kus'a" and "Uru" Dynasties from Indian Epics.[1]

Kus'a, founder of Kus'ā or Kus'ika Dynasty, s. of Balāka of Jahnu line.
Kus'āmba or Kus'ika, his son.
GĀDHI [*Gudia* or "*Gudea*"] his son.

Vis'wā-Mitra, son, became Sun-priest, who opposed human sacrifice.

Satya-watī, daughter, married sage Uru-Ricīka B'rigu.
Jama-Dagni the B'rigu, son, m. Renuka.
Paras'u-Ram, Rumanwat, SUSHENA, Vasu, Vis'wa-Vasu.

The following King-list of "Gudea's" (p. 59) and the "Ur" Dynasties from the Indian Epics,[2] compared with the names in the Sumerian King-lists and monuments, again shows how much more faithfully the Indian Epics have preserved these Sumerian names than those as "restored" by Assyriologists.

This comparison discloses among other things the Sumerian name for the founder of Gudia's dynasty was *Kus'* as recorded in the Indian Epics; and that the founder of the "Ur" Dynasty, *Uruas'zikum* of the Sumerian was *Uru-ricika* of the Indian Epics, which make him the son-in-law of Gadhi or Gudia.

It also would appear that "*Uruas'-nin Girsu*," the fourth on the list, the so-called king "Ur Ningirsu of Ur," was a *queen* and not a king. This position is occupied in the Epic list by the daughter of Gadhi (Gudia), whose personal name

[1] W.V.P., 4, 15 f., 28. [2] See note 1.

King-list of " Gudea's " and " Ur " Dynasties from Indian Epics compared with Sumerian.

Names in Indian Epics.	*Names in Sumerian*	
	As revised by me.	*As read by Assyriologists.*[1]
1. K'US'Ā, s. of Balāka.	Uru-as'-ba Kus'.	Ur-Bau.
2. Kus'ambha, s. of 1.	Khas'u [2]-ma'h-ia.	Nammakhni, s. of 1.
3. GĀDHI, s. of 2.	GU-DI-A.	GUDEA, s. of 2.
4. Satya-watī, daughter of 3.	Uru-as'-nin Gir-su.	Ur-Ningirsu, s. of 3.
5. *Uru-Ricika*, husb. of 4.	*Uru-as'-zikum.*	Ur - Nammu (Engur) founder of Ur Dynasty.
6. Jama-*Dagni*, s. of 4 and 5.	(S'amu) [3] *Duk-gin.*	*Dungi*, s. of 5.
7. *Paras'u* Rāma, s. of 6.	*Bur-as'-sin* (or *Pur-as'-sin*).	Bur Sin I., s. of 6.
8. SUSHENA, br. of 7.	S'U-AS'-SIN (or -en-zu)	Gimil Sin.

was Satya-watī, and who afterwards married the B'rigu priest Uru who founded the " Ur " Dynasty, and became the mother of Dungi. The title " Uru-as'-nin Girsu " means " The lady (*nin*) of *Uruas'* (a title of the solar angel Tasi) at Girsu "—Girsu being the suburb of Sirlapur, where were situated the chief temples. This would explain why Uruas'-nin-Girsu is found to be styled on monuments " *patesi* (or priest or priestess) of Sirpurla," as she was apparently the solar priestess there under her father Gudia ; it would also explain how (presumably after her marriage to Uru) she is styled " priestess of the god(dess) Ninā," and how

[1] *Cambridge Anc. Hist.*, Babylonia, 1924, *passim*.

[2] This word-sign in Sumerian has values *Sim* and *Nam* and one which is lost. As Akkadi synonym has *Khas'u*, I have adopted this value.

[3] Dukgin has the prefix *As'* " Lord "=" divine " or " heaven," which has Akkad value *S'amu*, which has evidently been adopted by the Sanskrit as not infrequent, thus showing " Semitic " influence.

she presented a beautiful carved votive-offering of a lady's coiffure in diorite to a "goddess," now in the British Museum. It would thus appear that Gudia, by his well-known over-zealous devotion to religion, made both his son (Viswāmitra) and daughter religious devotees, and so lost his kingdom for his dynasty.

"Bur Sin I.," properly *Buras'-Sin* or *Puras'-Sin*, is disclosed as the historical original of the fanatical reactionary *Paras'u Rāma* of the Indian Epics, who killed his mother (presumably a Sun-worshipper), and massacred the Sun-worshipping "Khattiyo" princes of the "Haryas'wa" and other contemporary dynasties. And he is still regarded as a popular hero amongst Indian Brahmans for raising the Brahman caste above the "Khattiyo" or ruler caste, by means of his axe, which he is represented in a common modern picture of his effigy as carrying (see Fig. 10); and his name *Paras'u* is rendered by Brahmans "axe." In calling the second part of his name *Rāma* instead of "Sin," it would seem that the later Indian Brahmans who edited the Epics intended "Rāma," ordinarily meaning in Sanskrit "dark, black, night," as a synonym for the Sumerian *Sin*, meaning "the Moon," of darkness, or to connote his "black" massacre.

Paras'u Rāma, although made by the later Brahmans a black incarnation of the Sun-god Vishnu, has little of Sun-worship is related of him. The hymn ascribed to him in the Vedas[1] is mainly an invocation of various female deities, including B'arati and Night and Morning; and also refers to his offering of human sacrifices,[2] which was abhorrent to Sun-worshippers. He is thus seen to have been a reactionary priest-king who incorporated in his religion the debasing matriarchal worship of the "Semitic" Chaldean aborigines with female deities and bloody sacrifices. This explains his massacre of the Sun-worshipping Haryas'was, and his in-

[1] R.V., 10, 110. [2] *Ib.*, v. 10.

veterate hostility to Gudia's son the solar priest Viswā-Mitra, who is specially represented in the Epics as opposing

FIG. 10.—Paras'u Rāma or "Rāma of the Axe" (Bur-as' Sin, or Pur-as' Sin I., of Ur Dynasty).
As slayer of Haryas'wa's line of Kings and exalter of Brahmans.
(After an eighteenth-century picture in Moor's *Hindoo Pantheon*.)

the human sacrifice of the Uru Dynasty. The records of "Bur-Sin I.," which are still extant on the monuments, are in keeping with this character; for although he repaired the ancient Sun-temple at Nippur he devoted his energies chiefly to the Moon cult and its goddesses at "Ur of the Chaldees," which is now being excavated with rich historical results by the joint expedition of the British Museum and the University of Pennsylvania under Mr. Wooley.

The name "Dungi" appears in the Indian Epics as "*Dagni*" with the prefix "Jama," so as to read "Jamadagni." This shows that the Sumerian name should be read *Duk-gin*,[1] though the later Brahmans seem to read into it some meaning by the Sanskrit word *Agni*, "Fire" (from the Sumerian *Ag* = "Fire within"), as Fire was an essential part of the B'rigus' cult. The prefix "Jama" apparently represents the Sumerian prefix *As'* usually employed by Dungi, and meaning, as we have seen in Mudgala's seal, "Lord" (also "divine and heaven"), and it has the Akkad synonym of *S'amu*; so that Dungi would appear to have been called by his Semitic, Chaldee subjects and by the Chaldee followers of his son Paras'u Rāma "*S'amu* Dukgin," from which the later Brahmans made "Jamadagni."

S'us'ēna of this seal is thus proved to be Sushena the second son of "Jamadagni" of the Indian Epics, and identical with King *S'u-sin* or *S'uas'-sin* or *S'uas'enzu* of the Ur Dynasty, and also identical with the "*S'us'ēna*" of the state of the Sus'a king afore-mentioned, especially as we find that King "S'u-sin" or "Suas'sin" of this Ur Dynasty was suzerain of Sus'a.[2] And he is disclosed in this seal with the title of "*Prince* of Gus'a" as governor during the lifetime of his father Dukgin,[3] of the tributary Edin district of the Indus Valley, about 2350 B.C. The finding of his signet in the fort of the Indus Valley, in view of the fact

[1] The sign "Dun" reads also "Du-*uk*" or *Dūk* (cp. B., 5912).
[2] His brick inscription was found at Sus'a (cp. K.H.S., 284).
[3] He is made *grandson* of Dungi by Assyriologists.

that he afterwards reigned as king of Ur in Mesopotamia, presumes that he had probably given it to a deputy-governor to stamp official documents, and it afterwards was preserved, like that of Sarogon I. (Seal VII.), as a royal heirloom there, in Edin.

The place-name on these seals with the Bull sign for "place or land or dwelling" is not always "Edin," as we have found in Seal IV. In this case though the two signs following the Bull very probably mean "Edin," they also may read "Ag-du" or "S'a-ki" Land, as seen in the decipherment table (Fig. 10). And we shall find that "S'āka Land" (the "Saki" of the Sumerian) was a title of the Indus Valley.

SEAL NO. VI.

Official Signet of TAX, "*minister of* SIRGANA *of Agdu*" (SARGON I. *of Agade*).

The Vedic and Indian Epic DAXA (*Dakska*) re S'AKUNI or *Sagara* of Ajodhya (as Sargon I. of Agade).

This small seal (Fig. 2, VI.), the finest of the series in artistic skill and technique, and thus presumably one of the later, is one of the most critically important historically of the whole series, for it appears with certainty to reveal, by the actual signet of his governor, the great world-emperor "*Sargon I. of Agade*" *as the suzerain of the Indus Valley about* 2800 B.C. *to* 2750 B.C.; just as we have found was Uruas'-the Khad through his son's seal. And we now realize for the first time fully the truth of the claim by Sargon in his contemporary monuments, wherein he styles himself "Emperor of the Four Quarters of the World," "Lord of the lands of the Lower Sea (Persian Gulf and Arabian Sea) and of the Upper or Western Sea (Mediterranean), and of the *Tin*-lands *beyond* the Western Sea"—the Tin-mines of the Cassiterides and Cornwall in Ancient Britain.[1]

[1] W.P.O.B., 160, 216 f., 413 f.

The critical word-signs here are those forming the two names of "*Sir-gun-a*" or "*Sa-gana*" for "Sargon I." and of "*Ag-du*" for "Agade" his capital. Their Sumerian word-signs with their phonetic values have been authenticated in the foregoing decipherment tables and foot-notes. If the place-name is "Edin" it is in series with the seal of Uruas' (or Ur-Ninā) as king of Edin.

The name "Sargon I." for the famous ancient world-emperor is adopted by Assyriologists in order to equate it with the Hebrew name for a later namesake, the Semitic Assyrian king "Sargon" of the Old Testament, who sent the Jews into captivity in the eighth century B.C. The ancient emperor, however, spelt his name on his own monuments, of which a few survive, as "*S'ar-gu-ni*" or *Sar-ga-ni* or "*Sir-gu-ni.*" And later *Semitic* scribes wrote his name as "*S'ar-ru-ki-in*" and *S'arru-gin*, in which latter the first syllabic sign is given its Akkadian Semitic value, from which it is assumed that Sargon I. was a Semite, instead of merely that the scribes themselves were Semites. For "Sargon I." we shall find was one of the most celebrated *Aryan* emperors, and an *Aryan Vedic king* like "Ur-Ninā," "Gudea," Dungi, Bur Sin, etc.

Over twenty years ago, I observed in comparing the Indian Epic lists of the Ancient Aryan kings with the Mesopotamian King-lists that the great Aryan king "*S'akuni*," occupied a relative position in the "Lunar" version of these lists corresponding to that of "*S'ar-gu-ni*" in the Mesopotamian King-lists. Moreover, the leading kings before and after Sargon I. were generally similar on both lists; and S'akuni's "son" or "descendant" was "*Karamb'a*," which suggested some resemblance to "*Naram-Sin*" of Assyriologists, who for long called him the "son" of "Sargon I.," though now he is found to be his grandson, and the most famous of Sargon's "sons" or descendants.

Later, on revising at first hand from the Sumerian and

cuneiform texts the readings of the Mesopotamian king's names as restored by Assyriologists, I found that the name read by them as " Naram Sin," also *reads by other recognized values for the syllabic signs of that king's name* " KA-RA-AM-BA," *and thus absolutely equates with the name in the Indian Epic King-lists for the " son " or " descendant " of*

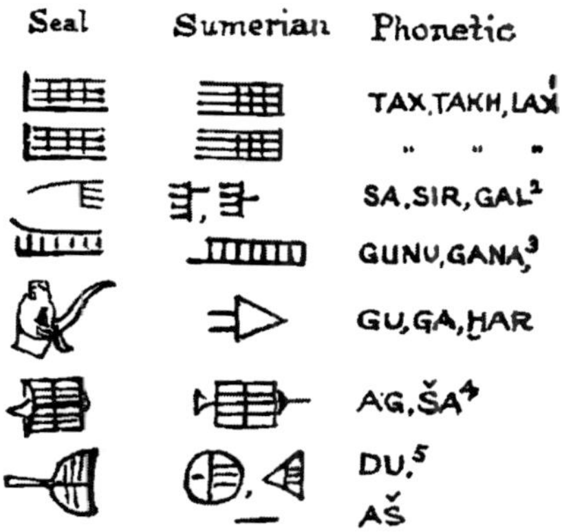

FIG. 11.—Signet Inscription of *Tax* (or " *Dax* ") minister of Sirgana of Agdu (Sargon I. of Agade).

Reads: Tax tax sa-(or *sir*)-gan-a (or gun-a) gu ag-du (or S'a-ki or Edin)-as'.

Transl.: *Tax,* the minister of *Sir-gana* (or Sa-guna) of the Land at (?) Agdu (or S'aki or Edin).

1. B.W., 278, Manis'tusu. *Tax* value, B., 6165.
2. This plumed Crown sign I have found with stem at one end several times (thus in Mudgala's seal, Fig. 5). On *Sa* value, B., 6839. It has also value *Sir,* cp. signs in definition in B., 6839, with 9519, and 9521.
3. This sign seems certain. It is a mannerism with the lapidary of this seal to not join up the transverse lines, cp. signs 1 and 2. On *gunu* value, M., 2011; and *kar,* B., 3813.
4. *Gu* or *'Har*=" Lands," see before.
5. This sign seems a variant of *du.* I have added for comparison sign T.D., 210; B.W., 355, value *Akh* (B., 8290), but it is unlikely, as it has no meaning of " fort, city or land " like the analogous sign on all the other seals.

King S'akuni. This identity was not confined merely to the external form of the name, but as I find *is usual in these Sanskrit names derived from the Sumerian, it extended also into the constituent syllables of this Sanskrit name.* Thus I observed that the syllabic word-sign *ba,* which in Sumerian has the meaning of " Moon," has in Sanskrit *ba* the meaning of "lunar mansion" and *b'ā* "to shine." And *Ka*, which has a Sumerian value of *Na*, meaning "no" or "not," is at least in the Akkadian a pronoun suffix, like the *Ka* in Sanskrit, which is a pronoun suffix especially in *negative* sentences, and also a suffix of diminution, *i.e.*, in a negative direction;[1] whilst *Na* in Sanskrit as in Sumerian = "no" or "not." Again *Am*(*a*) in Sanskrit means "strength,"[2] just as this *Am* or *Ama* in Sumerian means "strength."[3] Again *Ra* in Sanskrit = "acquiring,"[4] and in Sumerian = "seizing," *i.e.*, "acquiring."[5] Thus the identity of "Karamba" in Sumerian and Sanskrit is complete; and it shows that the authentic form of the name for Sargon's famous "son" or "descendant" is not "Naram Sin," but "*Karamba*."

Moreover, in the "Solar" (or Sun-worshippers') version of the Indian Epic lists of these Early Aryan kings, wherein the kings often bear different (solar) titles from those on the Lunar lists—parallel to the different and additional religious titles borne by the Ancient Egyptian kings as "son of the Sun"—in precisely the same relative position as occupied by S'akuni in the Lunar lists comes the great "world-emperor" SAGARA of *Ajodhya* or *Ayodhya*, the record of whose vast conquests generally resembles that of S'arguni or Sargon I. of Agade[6]—which latter city-name appears to be represented by the Ajodhya or Ayodhya of the Indian Epics.

This "Sagara" form of King S'arguni's (or Sargon's) name is actually found on his own Indus Valley seal, the next of the series (VII.). Now the "son" of *Sagara* in the Solar Indian Epics is "Asa-*Manjas*," who apparently corresponds to Sargon's eldest son the "*Manis'*-tis's'u or *Manis'*-tusu" of the Mesopotamian King-lists and inscriptions.[7]

The identity of "Sargon I." of Agade with the "*Sagunu*"

1 M.W.D., 240. 2 *Ib.*, 80. 3 M., 3059.
4 M.W.D., 859. 5 B., 6353. 6 W.V.P., 3, 291 f.
7 The prefix *Asa* means in Sanskrit "shining," and thus may represent the usual *As'* or "Lord" prefix in Sumerian kings' names, especially as that word-sign has pictograph of the rayed Sun, *i.e.* "the shining one," see Seal V.

or "*Sirgana*" of this Indus Valley seal on the one hand, and with the Aryan king *S'akuni* or *Sagara* of Ayodhya or Ajodhya of the Indian Epic King-lists on the other hand, is thus practically established.

The personal name of the "minister" owner of this seal, "*Tax*," identifies him probably with "Tax (or Dax)-the-Goth," the father of the owner of Seal No. VIII., and with the Indian Epic prince *Daxa*, son of Citrasena, son of Narishyanta of the Solar line, whose descendants are called *S'aka*,[1] *i.e.*, Sacæ or Getæ or Goths ; and thus would account for the owner of that seal (No. VIII.) being called "son of *Dax*," and being styled therein *Guti* or "Goth."

Two lines of descendants are ascribed to Narishyanta in the Epics, possibly owing to descent from two different sons. As the "son" of the Solar Manu, his descendants are Citrasena, *Daxa*, Mīdhuas (of Seal XIV.) and others to Satya-s'ravas[2] (of Seal XVIII. ?). Whilst as son of the Solar-line emperor Marutta (a Sumerian title for Morite or Amorite)[3] his descendants are Dama (of Seal VIII.) and others down to Trinabindu, father of Vis'āli ;[4] and Trinabindu was succeeded as "arranger of the Vedas" by a *Daxa*.[5]

From the agreement in the personal names in several of the following seals with those in the minor dynasty of Daxa's ancestor, Narishyanta, it seems possible that after Sargon's death the minister Tax of this seal, or his son, set up a petty independent or semi-independent dynasty in the Indus Valley, although they are nowhere called "king" on their seals. In this view, the Epic statement that the mythological Daxa (*i.e.*, Tascio) married the Asikni River,[6] *i.e.*, the Bias tributary of the Indus near Harappa, and that his descendants were called "Haryas'was,"[7] may be based on a memory of the presence of this Tax or Daxa minister of Sargon I.,

[1] W.V.P., 3, 336.
[2] *Ib.*, 3, 335.
[3] W.P.O.B., 216, 243 f.
[4] W.V.P., 3, 245.
[5] *Ib.*, 3, 335.
[6] *Ib.*, 2, 12.
[7] *Ib.*, 2, 12 f.

and of his sons in the Upper Indus Valley, and of his predecessor Sumerians there, the "*sons*" of Haryas'wa—the Sumerian emperor Uruas' (or "Ur-Ninā"), founder of the first Panch(-āla) or Phœnician Dynasty, with his capital at the seaport of Lagash or S'irlapur on the Persian Gulf.

"*Ag-du*" appears to be a possible reading of the place-name on this seal, rather than "S'a-ki" or "Edin." The composite sign for the latter name "Edin" we have seen consists of the three signs *Ga* or *Gu*, "dwelling-place" or "land," *Sir* (or E ?) and *Du* (or Dun ?); and that the initial *Ga* or *Gu*, "dwelling-place" or "land" evidently takes the place of the later prefix *Kur* "land" or *Uru* "city"; and that the name of this city proper as Agdu, S'aki or "Edin" is given in the last two word-signs. Treated in this manner we get for this word-sign the value *Ag-du*,[1] which would thus seem a dialectic form of "Agade," which is supposed to be the source of the later Assyrian "*Akkadu*." The previous seal of S'usēna may also have this same reading for its place-name.

Seal No. VII.

Official Signet of King Sagara, *or Sargon I. of Agade.*
The Epic King Sagara of Ayodhya.

This seal (Fig. 2, VII.) is of first-rate historical importance for both Indian and Mesopotamian history, as it is disclosed as the actual seal of the great emperor Sargon I. of Agade, under his solar Indian Epic title of "Sagara," as detailed under the previous seal of his "minister Tax."

It would appear that that great emperor, in the course of his world-wide conquests, actually visited his colony of Edin in the Indus Valley, or "S'āka Land," as it is called in the Indian Epics; and that he left his seal in the hands of

[1] The *Du* and *Ki* word-signs are almost indistinguishable in some of their early forms.

his governor there to stamp official documents. This would now explain more fully than has hitherto been known or suspected the real basis of fact on which Sargon I. claimed the title of " Lord of the Lower Sea " (the Persian Gulf and Indian Ocean).

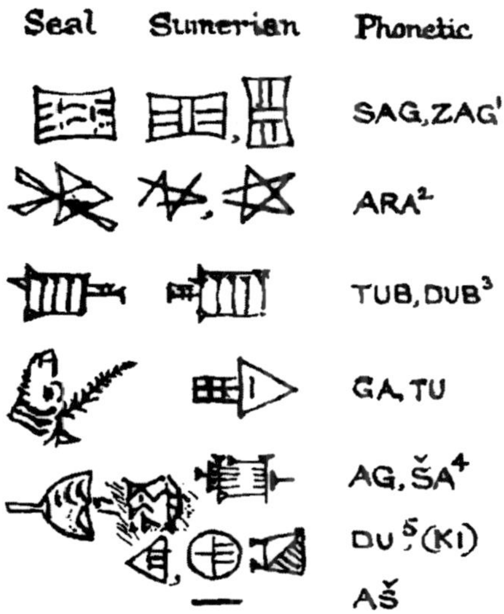

FIG. 12.—Signet Inscription of *Sagara* of *Agdu* (S'aki or Edin ?).

Reads : Sag-ara dub gu-ag-du (or S'a-ki or edin)-as'.
Transl. : *Sagara*, the tablet of, at land of *Agdu* (or S'aki or *Edin*).

1. Sumer sign, T.D., 176; B.W., 291. *Sag* "prince," B., 6461 ; with Akkad value *S'arru* " king "; B., 6503—*i.e.*, same value as first part of Sargon or S'aru-kin's name.
2. T.D., 177 ; B.W., 261. *Ara* value, B., 5775.
3. B.W., 157 ; T.D., 385. *Dup* " tablet " = Akkad *Tuppu*, B., 3935.
4. This may read either *Ag* or *SA*.
5. May read either *Du* or KI.

The place-name here appears to have as its first sign the word-sign *Ag* or *S'a*, rather than that of " Edin " ; whilst the second sign may read either *du* or *ki*, in which these form an essential portion of the place-name, and not mean merely " fort " or " land " or " city," as the " land " or " dwelling " element is the first sign *Ga* or *Gu*. In favour of the reading *S'aki* is the fact which we have seen that this was a Sumerian name for the "Edin temple of the Slave-girl," and it is clearly the equivalent of the Indian Epic *S'āka* or "The Land of the S'akas," an Epic title of the Indus Valley, as seen later on.

There is, moreover, the fact recorded of King Sagara in the Indian Epics that he conquered the S'akas.[1] And it is further recorded therein that as a punishment, "he compelled the S'akas to shave the (upper) half of their heads,"[2] an outrageous punishment for a people who prided themselves as the Sacæ or Goths did in their long locks.

Seal No. VIII.

Official Signet of Damu (*or* Gudama) *the Guti or "Goth"* son of Dax the 'Har(-ri).

The Epic Dama of the *Daxa* line of *S'akas* (or Goths).

This seal (Fig. 2, VIII.) appears to be the signet of "The Warrior *Damu*," who was probably identical with the Epic prince *Dama* of the line of Daxa the S'aka, referred to in the notes on Seal VI., and who was possibly the owner of that seal.

The personal name as seen from the decipherment table may read "The warrior *Damu*," and this appears to be the reading intended, in view of the patronym *Dax* and the ethnic title "*Guti*" or "Goth." If the first word-sign *Gu* is taken as the first syllable of the name, the latter would read *Gudamu*, which equates with the Vedic and Epic name "Gotama," a title of the seer Dīrgha-tamas (or "Aus'ija"), who has been referred to in Seals I. and IV.; and whose descendants, the Aus'ijas, were also called "Gotamas," and are found in the Indus Valley seals; and the name is spelt "Go*d*ama" in the Burmese Pali, as the family name of Buddha, the seer of the S'akya tribe. "*Gādama*" (as

[1] W.V.P., 3, 291 f. [2] *Ib.*, 292.

"Gāmdama" with its nasal *m* must have read earlier) was the name of a man in Vedic literature, who bore the title of "Eka-Yāvan,"[1] *i.e.*, "The Ionian," and thus was presumably an early Goth.

His patronym of *Dax* or *Tax* equates with name of the

FIG. 13.—Signet Inscription of *Damu* the *Guti* son of *Dax* the 'Har(-ri).
Reads: Gu(t)-damu gu-ti mar-dax (or *-tax*) gut (or har).
Transl.: The warrior *Damu*, the *Guti* son of *Dax* (or Tax), the 'Har(-ri).

1. This sign of the Egg and Chicken (or Goose) is written in Sumerian with egg outside chicken, see col. 2, from T.D., 36; B.W., 88. It has meaning of "bear children, family or kin" and ordinary value *Mūt* or *Mud*. But it has Akkad value of *Dāmu* "family or kin" (B., 2276–7); and *Damu* is Sumerian for "child, son and daughter." It is thus probable that this sign had the *Damu* value also in Sumerian. In any case the Sanskrit, I find, frequently adopts the Akkad value of Sumerian words (W.P.O.B., 324, etc.); and this *Damu* value brings it into relation with the Dax patronym of the seal.
2. This "Son" sign of a young animal in Sumerian, in col. 2, is from Khamurabi's Code, B.W., 392.
3. Sumer sign, T.D., 59; B.W., 182, period of Lugalzag.

owner of the previous seal (VI.), and with the personal name Daxa of the Vedas and Epics. In Vedic literature is a prince named Daxa, surnamed "The Hill-man" (Pārvati), and two teachers of that name,[2] and in the Epics also is a Vedic teacher Daxa,[3] who may be one of these. Thus his

[1] Cp. M.K.I., 1, 118, 226.
[2] *Ib.*, 335.
[3] W.V.P., 3, 35, 111.

patronym along with his ethnic title of Guti appears to identify him with *Dama*, the "descendant" or "son" of Narishyanta the S'aka (or Goth) before mentioned, of whom Daxa was also a descendant.

Of this Dama, descendant of Narishyanta, it is related in an Epic [1] that his bride Sumanā, daughter of King Dasarha, was rescued by him from his rivals, one of whom, Vapush-mat, in revenge killed the grandfather of Dama, named Marutta, who had relinquished his kingdom and retired into hermitage. Thereon Dama slew Vapush-mat and offered the body to the manes of his "father" as an obsequial offering.

His tribal or ethnic title of Guti or "Goth" is of great historical importance as conclusively attesting his Aryan racial character, and the presence of Goths in the Indus Valley about 2750 B.C.

Seal No. IX.

Official Signet of As's'ias' *the Kaz(-zi) at Edin.* Vedic Aus'ija the *Kās'i* (?).

This "As's'ias' the Kaz" of this seal (Fig. 2, IX.) is apparently a different member of the Aus'ija family of priests from "As's'ias' the Khās' (or 'seer')" of Seal I., who bore the title of "Barugu" or B'rigu Fire-priest.

"*Kaz*" appears to be his clan title of "Kazzi," a recognized Phœnician form of "Kassi," see Chap. X. And the Aus'ijas were of the Kās'i line.

The place-name may be "Edin," as before, or "S'aki" (or Agdu); but the cylindrical sign seems open at the top, and thus resembles the *Si* or *Sig* sign as shown in the table. It cannot well be the sign "Daxa," as this has no stem.

[1] W.V.P., 3, 245.

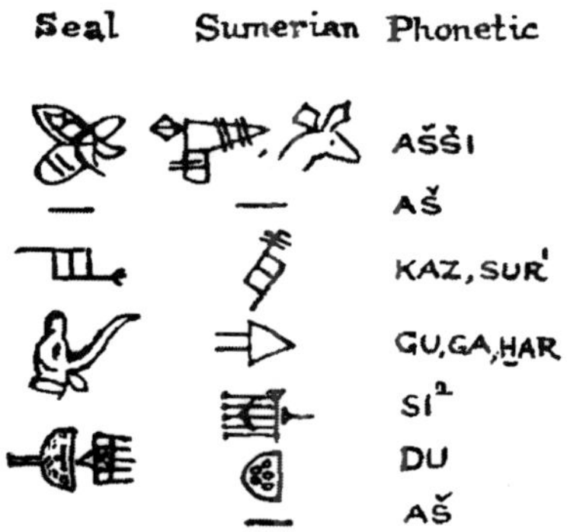

FIG. 14.—Signet Inscription of *As's'ias'* the *Kaz* at Edin(?).
Reads : As's'i-as' kaz edin (?)-as'.
Transl. : *As's'ias'* the *Kaz*(-*zi*) at Edin(?).

1. B.W., 364A, pl. 169. On *Kaz* value, M., 6540.
2. B.W., 308 and 321 with *Si* and *Sig* values.

SEAL NO. X.

Official Signet of KAN(-WA ?) S'AR . . . *of S'iki* (*S'ug-ki*). The Vedic KANWA S'RAYASA (?).

In this fragment of seal (Fig. 2, X.), a considerable portion of the inscription is lost, but the initial portion shows it was the seal of a Kan(-wa) Fire-priest.

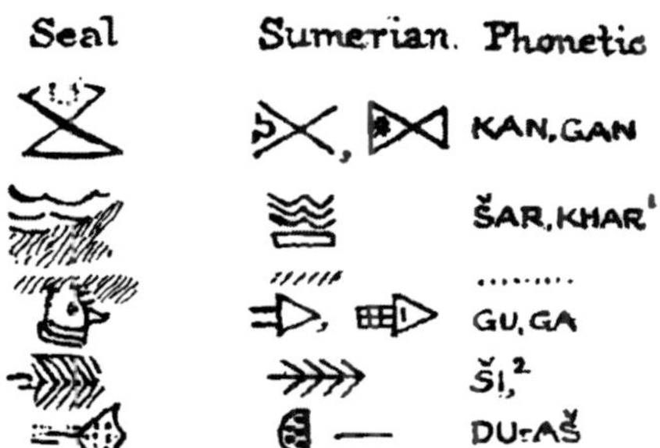

FIG. 15.—Signet Inscription of *Kan*(-*wa* ?) *S'ar* . . . of S'iki (or Sugki).
Reads : Kan s'a . . . gu-s'i-ki (s'ug-ki)-as'.
Transl. : *Kan*(-*wa* ?) *S'ar* . . . at *S'iki*(?).

1. This seems the *S'ār* sign, B.W., 170, Manis'tusu.
2. This seems variant of Wheat-ear sign, B.W., 323. The Sumer sign in col. 2 is of " Ur-Ninā " period.

This probably is the seal of Kanwa S'rayasas, a Vedic sage mentioned in Vedic literature.[1]

The place-name appears to read *S'iki* or *S'ugki*. This may be a dialectic variant of *S'aki*, the "S'aka Land" of the Lower Indus. "S'ikhi" is a variant of *S'ibi* in the Indian Epics.[2]

SEAL NO. XI.

Official Signet of S'ar-gad GAL-'HA *the Bargu or B'rigu Fire-priest.*

The Indian Epic priest GĀLAWA the *B'rigu.*

This partly broken small seal (Fig. 2, XI.) reads clearly (except in regard to the last word-sign, which also, however,

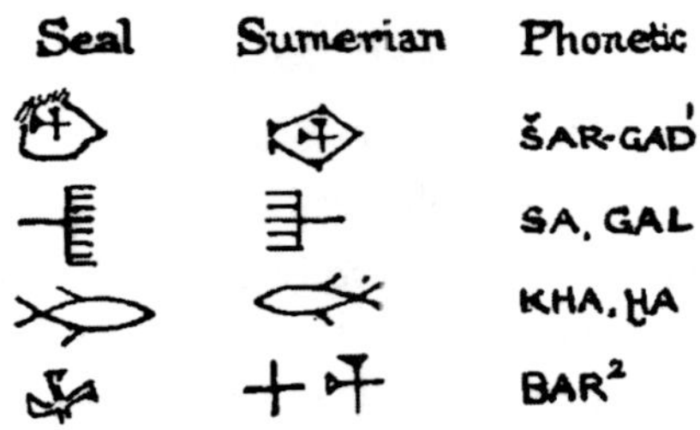

FIG. 16.—Signet Inscription of S'ar-gad *Gal'ha*, the B'rigu.
Reads: S'ar-gad gal-'ha bar-gu.
Transl.: S'ar-gad *Gal'ha* the Bargu or B'rigu.

1. B.W., 364 B. Value *S'ar-gad*, B. 12221.
2. T.D., 29; B.W., 77.

seems fairly certain) "S'ar-gad Gal-'ha Bar-gu." It thus appears to be the seal of the Indian Epic priest Gālawa the B'rigu of the Kus'ika line, who is associated with Paras'u Rāma[3] of that line, see before. S'ar-gad may mean "King of the *Gad* (*i.e.*, Phœnicians)" or "King Gadhi," *i.e.*, Gudia or Gudea. In either case this B'rigu appears to have been the family priest of a king, Phœnician or otherwise,

[1] M.K.I., 1, 134.
[2] W.V.P., 3, 7.
[3] *Ib.*, 2, 113; 3, 23.

" Gadhi," we have seen was also of the Kus'ika line. On the title *Gad* for " Phœnician," see seal, No. XIII.

The swastika form of the *Bar* sign, +, will be noticed.

SEAL No. XII.

Official Signet of S'ABTAR . . . *of Edin.*
Epic SAVITRI (?) Vedic teacher.

This defaced and scaled seal (Fig. 2, XII.) is illegible in considerable parts of its legend; but its first two signs are distinct, especially the first. These read *S'ab-tar* and

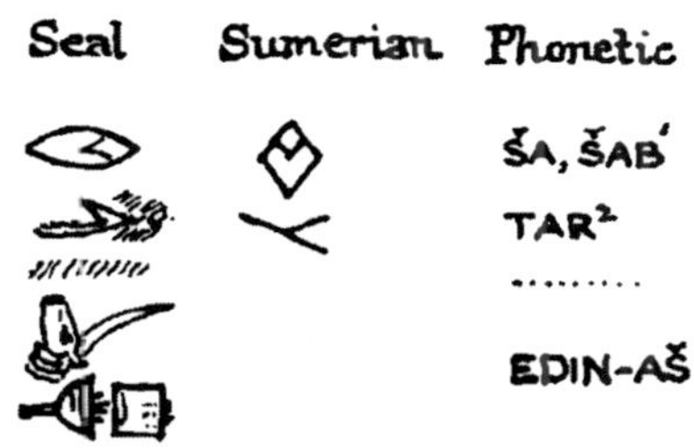

FIG. 17.—Signet Inscription of *S'abtar* of Edin.

Reads : S'abtar . . . edin-as'.
Transl. : *S'abtar* . . . at Edin.

1. T.D., 255 ; B.W., 340, " Eannatum," where chevron first appears.
2. T.D., 123 ; B.W., 12.

apparently identify this personage with the subject of the Death-Amulet Seal No. XVIII., which see.

The name *S'abtar* equates fairly well with the Sanskrit *Savitri*, the name of a teacher who " arranged the Vedas " in the fifth age ;[1] and a Savitri who was the grandson of the mythic Daxa ;[2] whilst *Sāvitrī* was a daughter of that Daxa.[3] The two latter may thus be derived from the historical owner of this seal and grafted on to the mythic Daxa by the later Indian myth-mongering Brahmans.

This Sumerian seal name *Sabtar*, meaning literally " Heart " (*S'ab*) + " decide, look after "[4] (*tar*), appears to

[1] W.V.P., 3, 34 f.
[2] *Ib.*, 2, 27.
[3] *Ib*, 2, 21.
[4] B., 381 ; M., 316.

disclose the Sumerian source and meaning of the Sanskrit "*Savitri*," "the vivifier or enlivener," as "looker after the heart," as a title applied to the God behind the Sun as the "vivifier."

The remaining two fragments of seals, which are obviously signets, as distinguished from Death-Amulets, although containing the bull and in one case the "Edin" designation, want altogether the portion bearing the personal name or title.

FIG. 34.—Buras' Sin or Puras' Sin, Paras'u Rāma, exterminating the Haryas'was.
(After an eighteenth-century picture from Moor's *Hindoo Pantheon*.)

VIII

Death-Amulet Indo-Sumerian Seals from Mohenjo Daro and Harappa deciphered and translated

Disclosing owners as Aryan Sumerian Vedic and Indian Epic priests, priestesses and princes; Amulets for Resurrection from the Dead by Sun; Formulas identical with Amorite Phœnician "Cup-marked" Inscriptions in Ancient Britain; and Sumerian origin and meaning of Indian Sun-god Vishnu.

These Sumerian Death-Amulet seals from the Indus Valley (see Fig. 3), forming as they do a class apart from the official signets, are treated here separately, and are numbered in consecutive order with the signets for reference. Like the second series of signets from the Indus Valley, there is so far no record published as to which of them were found at Mohenjo Daro and which at Harappa.

The discovery that the Sumerian "Sun-worshippers" made free use of Death-Amulet seals in order to procure Resurrection from the Dead by means of the "Resurrecting" Sun has been announced and detailed in my former work with numerous illustrated and translated examples—not only from the Sumerians, but also from the Hitto-Phœnicians and Amorites and their Trojan branch, and from the Morite Phœnicians as recorded in the prehistoric Cup-marked inscriptions in Early Britain.[1]

[1] W.P.O.B., 236 f.

Although such Sumerian Death-Amulets with their prayers for Resurrection are, as I have observed, common amongst the Sumerians and have been unearthed in considerable numbers in Mesopotamia and Susa (" Elam ") and on Hitto-Phœnician seals, they nevertheless have not hitherto been recognized as such by Assyriologists, who have tried to read their "numeral" script as mere numbers, and thus have been misled into conjecturing these Death-Amulet seals and tablets to be merely "temple accounts" of supposed votive gifts of specified numbers of articles or animals to the Sun or other deity, though such "readings" have signally failed to yield any very consistent or intelligible results.[1]

These Death-Amulets of the Sumerians in the Indus Valley now *confirm my former readings of this " Cup-mark " Sumerian numeral script, and thus confirm my discoveries regarding the Sumerian origin and phonetic sacred values and readings of the Cup-mark script on the prehistoric monuments and grave-stones of Ancient Britain, and on the Sumero-Phœnician racial origin of the Goths and Britons, as well as the Indo-Aryans.*

The outstanding feature of the script on these Death-Amulet seals, it will be noticed, is the presence *in each* of them of vertical strokes, in series of threes and upwards, *which are entirely absent in the signets.* These vertical strokes represent the Sumerian numeral notation, which in the archaic lapidary Sumerian script was represented by drilled *Cup-marks* or circular depressed cups, and not strokes, as already noted in Chap. IV. The manner in which the Early Sumerians apparently came to use these numerical cup-marks and series of strokes, from one upwards, as a sacred mystical script with definite ideographic values for The One Universal Father-god Induru or Bel (1 or unity), the Sun (2, for Day and Night or " Resurrecting " Sun), the Dead (3) and so on, is fully detailed in my former work in the chapter on " Sumerian Cup-mark Script."

[1] *E.g.*, J.A.O.S., 23, 19 f.

The formulas inscribed on these Indus Valley Death-Amulets, significantly are seen to be couched in the same general form, with the same divine names, as those which I have previously translated from Sumerian, Hitto-Phœnician, Trojan and Morite Phœnician Death-Amulets, and the Cup-marked tombstones of Ancient Britain. They invoke for resurrection from the dead, by the Resurrecting Sun, the aid of the Father-god Induru (Indra, " Ia " or Bel), or his solar archangel Tax (Tascio or St Michael, " Ningirsu "), " The Sun-Fish " or the Sun itself, as in the amulets I have formerly translated. And it will be seen that the supposititious Sumerian " goddess Ninā " of Prof. Sayce and others is the Resurrecting Sun-Fish divinity invoked on these seals, and identical in form and name with the Indian Sun-god Vishnu.

As such Death-Amulets were usually tied to the dead bodies of the persons respectively named therein, or buried alongside their bodies or ashes, the unearthing of these Death-Amulets in such numbers during the excavation of these two Indus Valley sites presumes that the actual tombs of the persons therein named—including Early Vedic and Epic priests, priestesses and princes—were exhumed during these excavations. A photograph of one of these masonry tombs at Mohenjo Daro [1] shows that the body, as usual with the Early Sumerians, was buried in a " hunched " or contracted position—the body being laid on its side with the face turned towards the rising Sun. Similarly, the finding of so many signets also presumes that some of them also were exhumed from the tombs of their owners.

The *Script* on these Death-Amulets is of the same Sumerian type as on the signets, with the addition of the higher series of the Sumerian numeral script. An especially interesting sign is the wavy line with two other associated lines in Seal XIV. (Fig. 19). It evidently represents the three

[1] M.R., 529.

wavy lines found on Early Sumerian, Phœnician and Trojan Death-Amulets and on the Cup-marked "prehistoric" monuments of Ancient Britain.[1] It has the word-value of *Kus* or *Lum*, meaning "the Cut off (dead)," or "Crouched up (dead)," [2] which latter may refer to the crouched up position in which the Sumerians and Early Aryans buried their dead.[3]

The Language on these Death-Amulets, as on the signets, is standard Sumerian of the same condensed early agglutinative type with a minimum of grammatical elements.

Like the signets, as the photographs of these amulet "seals" are direct and not from impressions, they require to be turned on their right side for decipherment, which gives the word-signs in reversed form, as seen from column 2 of the decipherment tables.

Seal No. XIII.

Death-Amulet Seal of Uggu *the "Gad," "Kad" or "Phœnician."*

The Vedic (?) Uccaih king of *Kuru-Panch*(-ālas) or "Syrio-Phœnicians."

This amulet seal (Fig. 3, XIII.) is of immense historical significance if, as seems almost certain, it discloses the wearer as a celebrated Vedic king of the Kuru-Panch(-āla) or Syrio-Phœnicians, and the Early Vedic kings were *ex officio priest*-kings or seers. It moreover employs the title "*Gad*" or "*Kad*" (as in Seal XI.) for "Phœnician"—and a title which I have shown was a favourite one of the latter.[4]

[1] W.P.O.B., 15, 238 f., 249, 308.

[2] M., 8564, 8567–8.

[3] It was formerly read by me in my translations of Amulets as "multitude of waters" (W.P.O.B., 255 f.), in accordance with its usually supposed pictograph; but now is seen to mean "cut off" or "crouched up," like a "bunch of withered grass."

[4] W.P.O.B., 18, 74 f., 200 f.

It thus supplies direct evidence for the presence of Phœnicians in the Indus Valley about 3000 B.C.

It also discloses the Sumerian origin and meaning of the Indian Vedic name "Vishnu" for the Sun-god, and the

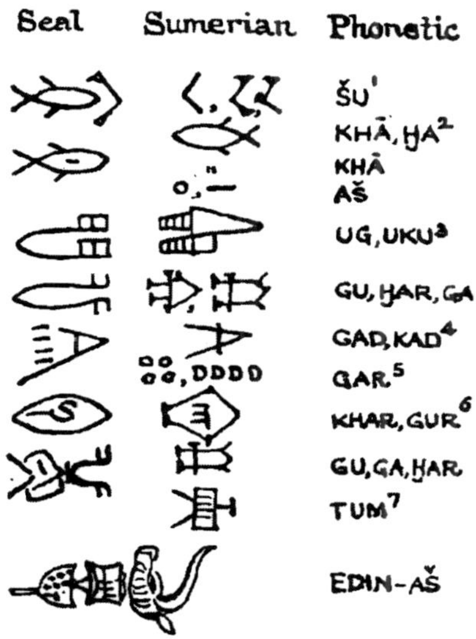

FIG. 18.—Amulet Inscription of *Uggu* the *Gad* or *Kad* (or Phœnician).

Reads: S'u-khā kha-as' uk-gu gad gar gur (or Khar) gu-tum edin-as'.
Transl.: O Setting-Sun Fish! the sage *Uggu* the *Gad* lift up from grave, bring to Life, at Edin.

1. T.D., 257; B.W., 365 and 490. Setting Sun with value *S'u*.
2. Fish sign as before.
3. T.D., 183; B.W., 150. "A horned wild animal," M.D., 58. *Ug* or *Uk* (B., 3860)=? source of our English word "Ox" and Sanskrit *Uksan* "Ox."
4. T.D., 178; B.W., 101. *Gad* or *Kad*, B., 2701.
5. *Gar*, B.W., 433, pl. 112, and W.P.O.B., 243 f.
6. B.W., 361, *Gur*, *Khar* (B., 8514–6)="box, receptacle, lie down, pit" (B., 8586, etc., and M., 6428 f.)=our English "Grave."
7. T.D., 167; B.W., 390. *Tum*="Life," M., 6816.

name "Sukhā" for the Western Ocean paradise of the Sun-god in Brahmanist and Buddhist myth.

On "The Fish of the Setting Sun," which is here invoked for Resurrection from the Dead, and its pictorial representation on ancient Sumerian and Hitto-Phœnician sacred seals and on Ancient Briton monuments, see my former work,[1] of which the results therein announced are now confirmed and established by the evidence of these Indo-Sumerian seals.

This Sumerian " Fish " title for the Sun-god on this and the other amulet seals, as " Fish of the Setting Sun (*S'u-khā*) " is of the utmost critical importance for establishing the Sumerian origin of the Indo-Aryans, and the Aryan character of the Sumerian language, as it discloses for the first time the origin and hitherto unknown real meaning of the Vedic name for the Sun-god " Vishnu," and of his representative as a Fish-man, as well as the Sumerian origin of the English word " Fish," the Gothic " Fisk " and Latin " Piscis."

The first " incarnation " of the Sun-god Vishnu in Indian mythology is represented as a Fish-man (see Fig. 19), and in substantially the same form as the Sumerian Fish-man personification of the Sun-god of the Waters in the Sumerian seals.

Now the Sumerians of Mesopotamia called the Setting Sun " The Fish (*Khā*) " [2]—a fact which has not hitherto been remarked or recognized. And this Sumerian title of " Fish " for the Sun is explained in the bilingual Sumero-Akkadian glossaries by the actual word occurring in this and the other Indo-Sumerian amulets, namely *S'u-khā*, with the addition of " man " (*na*),[3] by word-signs which read literally " The Winged Fish-man " ; [4] thus co-relating the Winged or soaring Sun with the Fish personification of the supposed " returning or resurrecting " Sun in " the waters under the earth." This solar title of " The Winged Fish " is further given the synonym of " The turning *Bi-i-i-es'*," [5] which latter name

[1] W.P.O.B., 247 f., 251, 308.
[2] B., 8638. [3] *Ib.*, and 1586.
[4] *S'u*=" wing," B.W., 311.
[5] Gar-bi-i-i-es' (B., 7244) ; *gar*=" turn " (B., 11984) ; *es'* (B., 2551).

is evidently a variant spelling of the Sumerian *Pi-es'* or ***Pish*** for "Great Fish" with the pictograph word-sign of

FIG. 19.—Sumerian Sun-Fish as Indian Sun-god Vishnu.

From an eighteenth-century Indian image (after Moor's *Hindoo Pantheon*).

Note the Sun-Cross pendant on his necklace. He is given four arms to carry his emblems: (*a*) Disc of the Fiery Wheel (weapon) of the Sun, (*b*) Club or Stone-mace (Gadā or Kaumo-dakī) [1] of the Sky-god Varuna, (*c*) Conch-shell (S'ank-ha), trumpet of the Sea-Serpent demon,[2] (*d*) Lotus (Padma) as Sun-flower.[3]

1. Significantly this word "Kaumo-dakī" seems to be the Sumerian *Qum*, "to kill or crush to pieces" (B., 4173; B.W., 193) and *Dāk* or *Daggu* "a cut stone" (B., 5221, 5223).

2. "Protector of the S'ankha (or Conch)" is the title of the first and greatest Sea-Serpent king in Buddhist myth, see my List of Nāga (or Sea-Serpent) Kings in *Jour. Roy. Asiat. Soc.*, Jan. 1894.

3. On the Lotus as symbol of heavenly birth, see my W.B.T., 338, 381, 388.

Fish joined to sign "great." [1] This now discloses the Sumerian origin not only of the "*Vish*" in Vish-nu, but also of the English "Fish," Latin "Piscis," etc.—the labials B, P, F and V being freely interchangeable in the Aryan family of languages. The affix *nu* in "Vish-nu" is obviously the Sumerian *Nu* title of the aqueous form of the Sun-god S'amas and of his father-god Ia or In-duru (Indra) as "God of the Deep." [2] It literally defines them as "The lying down, reclining or bedded" (god) [3] or "drawer or pourer out of water." [4]

It thus explains the common Indian representation of Vishnu as reclining upon the Serpent of the Deep amidst the Waters, and also seems to disclose the Sumerian origin of the Ancient Egyptian name *Nu* for the "God of the Deep." [5] Thus the name "Vish-nu" is seen to be the equivalent of the Sumerian *Pish-nu,* and to mean "The reclining Great Fish(-god) of the Waters"; and it will doubtless be found in that full form in Sumerian when searched for. And it would seem that this early "Fish" epithet of Vishnu for his "first incarnation" continued to be applied by the Indian Brahmans to that Sun-god even in his later "incarnations" as the "striding" Sun-god in the heavens. Indeed the Sumerian root *Pish* or *Pis* for "Great Fish" still survives in Sanskrit as *Vis*-āra "fish." [6] This name thus affords another of the many instances which I

[1] On sign T.D., 139; B.W., 303. The sign is called "Increased Fish" (*Kua-gunu, i.e., Khā-ganu,* B., 6925), in which significantly the Sumerian grammatical term *gunu* meaning "increased" as applied to combined signs, is radically identical with the Sanskrit grammatical term *guṇa* (="multiplied or auxiliary," M.W.D., 357) which is applied to the increased elements in bases forming diphthongs, and thus disclosing also the identity of Sanskrit and Sumerian grammatical terminology.

[2] M., 6741, 6759; B., 8988.

[3] B., 8990–1, 8997.

[4] *Ib.*, 8993.

[5] This *Nu* is probably a contraction for *Nun,* or "Great Fish," a title of the god Ia (or Induru) of the Deep (B., 2627). Its Akkad synonym of *Naku,* as "drawer or pourer out of Water," appears cognate with the Anu(n)-*naki*, or "Spirits of the Deep," and with the Sanskrit *Nāga* or "Sea-Serpent."

[6] M.W.D., 1000. The affix *ara* is presumably the Sanskrit affix *ra,* added to roots to form substantives, just as in Sumerian the affix *ra* is similarly added (cp., L.S.G., 81).

have found of the Sumerian origin of Aryan words, and in particular in the Sanskrit and English.

This Fish-man form of the Sumerian Sun-god of the Waters of the Deep, Piesh, Pish or Pis (or Vish-nu), also appears to disclose the unknown origin of the name of the Greek Sea-god "*Pos*-eidōn," the Neptune of the Romans (see Fig. 20). That name now seems to mean "The Likeness (*eidōn*) of *Pos*," *i.e.*, Pis or Piesh, "The Great Fish";

FIG. 20.—Pos-eidōn of the Greeks as the Sumerian Sun-Fish god *Pis* or *Bēiesh*.
From Greek vase painting of fifth century B.C.

and thus discloses the derivation of that Greek name and myth from the Sumerian. Moreover, the second part of that Greek name, *eidōn*, as well as its cognates in the Aryan family of languages, are also clearly derived from the Sumerian. In Sumerian *Bi-ad* = "see, look, form."[1] Now in Early Greek *eidōn* is spelt *Fid*-on, "see or look," and is cognate with the Latin *Vid*-eo, the Sanskrit *Vid* or *Ved*, "know," Gothic *Vit* and English "to *wit*" and "*wit*-ness"; and thus again is disclosed the Sumerian origin of Aryan words.

[1] *Bi-ad*, B., 9258; *Bi*, value, B., 103.

Further and complete identification of this Sumerian solar divinity or angel of Induru (Indra), "The Setting Sun-Fish," with Vishnu is had in the Sumerian tradition which connotes "Three" and "Steps" with the Winged Sun-Fish and "The Great Fish"; and thus discloses the Sumerian origin of the Indian Vedic tradition frequently referred to that Vishnu takes "Three Steps." In the Sumerian definition of the Setting Sun as a "Fish" we find the Sun described as "The *Stepping* Fish-man";[1] and

FIG. 21.—Vishnu as Sun-Fish man (*S'ukha* or *Btesh*) in Assyrio-Babylonian monuments. (After Layard.)

S'ukhā or "The Winged Fish" is defined as "*Bi-i-i-esh*," which is obviously a variant spelling of *Pi-esh* or *Pish* or "Great Fish." And this latter word has also the secondary meaning of "Three,"[2] presumably from fish occurring in swarms, and "three" was an early primitive expression for "a large number."[3] These "Three Steps" of the Sun-god Vishnu are thus seen to be the three steps or stages of the Sun's supposed daily progress: (1) upwards from the horizon of sunrise to the zenith, (2) downwards from the

[1] *Gir-kha-na*, B., 8638. *Gir*="step" (B., 9185). This has been arbitrarily rendered "eserit" and "madutu" of the Semitic.
[2] B., 6938. [3] Cp. P.S.L., 269.

zenith to sunset, and (3) the supposed retrograde or "resurrecting" stage as a Fish, from west to east, through "the waters under the earth" to the point of sunrise.

This now recovers for us the explanation, personality and hitherto unknown name of the common Assyrio-

FIG. 22.—Sun-Fish-man (*S'ukha* or *Btesh*) bestowing the ambrosia of Resurrection and Life, in Assyrio-Babylonian monuments. (After Layard.)

Babylonian images of the Fish-man divinity traversing the waters (Fig. 21), or carrying a basket and bestowing the Life-giving ambrosia of Resurrection (Fig. 22). On his name as the so-called "goddess Ninā" (see App. II.). This Sun-Fish divinity of the Resurrection and the Life of the old Aryan gentiles seems also the source of the title "The Fish" applied to Christ by the early Christian fathers, and his symbol as such is usually represented facing eastwards like the Sumerian and Hittite Sun-Fish-god.

This "S'ukhā" name for the Resurrecting Sun-Fish is apparently the Sumerian source of the Sanskrit name *Sukhā* for "heaven" and for "the western paradise of the God of the Deep" (Varuna), who is represented in Indian mythology as a Fish-man, as in the Sumerian seals of this Sun-Fish, or as riding upon a Fish. This Resurrecting Sun-Fish name "S'ukhā," seems also to disclose the Sumerian origin and unknown meaning of the Sanskrit mystic invocation and amulet word "*Swāhā*," so common in Brahmanism and on Buddhist amulets; [1] through the later dialectic dropping out of the *k* in the guttural *kh* of the *khā*, whereby *Khatti* became "*H*atti" (or "Hitt-ite") and Khamurabi became "*H*amurabi"; and thus "S'u-khā" became "*S'uhā*" and "*Swāhā*." [2]

The personal name *Uggu* equates fairly well with the Vedic *Uccaih*-"the famous" (Uccaih-s'ravas) surnamed Kaupayeya, who was a king of the Kurus,[3] and a maternal uncle of the Panch(-āla) or Phœnician prince Kes'in Darbhya. The Kurus and Panch(-ālas) are repeatedly referred to as kinsmen and allies under a joint king.[4] This would explain the *Gad* or *Kad* title in the seal; and this Gad or early Gothic personal name Uggu is probably the original of the latter Aryan personal name aspirated as "Hugo."

The Sumerian word-sign here for "grave," *Gur* or *Khar*, is defined as "box, receptacle, slay, lie down, dig," and thus seems to be the origin of our English word "grave." In the Akkadian the sign is called *Khāra*, also *Kapru* (presumably cognate with *Kaparu*, "cover, destroy"),[5] and

[1] W.B.T., 405 f.

[2] This "Swāhā" so common an invocation in the mouths of Brahmans is merely called "the calling to the gods," and by later Brahmans is supposed to be the name of the wife of the Fire-god.

[3] M.K.I., 1, 84, 187. Thus the first historical king of the Ganges Valley, already referred to, is described as King of the Kuru-Panch(-ālas).

[4] M.D., 403.

[5] W.P.O.B., 54.

thus presumably the origin of the late Phœnician *Khabr* or *Qabr*, "a grave," and the Gothic *Kubl*, and English "cover."

SEAL No. XIV.

Death-Amulet Seal of MIDAS'.

The Epic MĪDHWAS, " son " of *Daxa* the *S'aka*.

This important seal (Fig. 3, XIV.) supplements and confirms the reading of several of the preceding signet seals

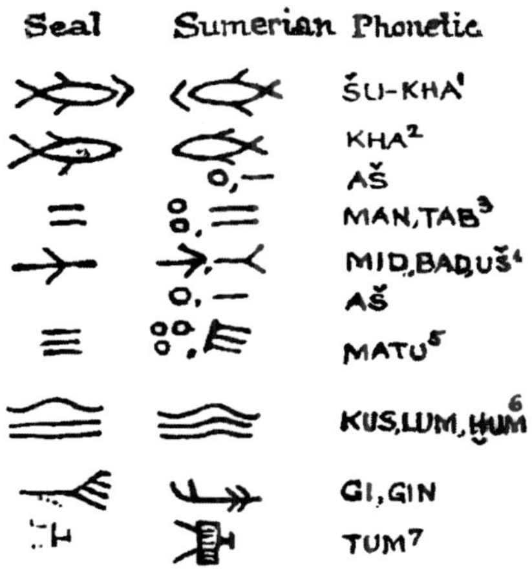

FIG. 23.—Amulet Inscription of *Midas'*.

Reads : S'u-kha kha-as'-buzur mid-as' matu kus gin tum.
Transl. : O Setting-Sun-Fish ! The seer of the Sun, *Midas'* the dead one, the cut off, bring to Life !

1. See previous Fig.
2. See previous Fig.
3. On this sign for the Sun as a dual with phonetic value of *Buzur*, *Man* or *S'amas'*, see footnote to Fig. 8 (Seal IV.) ; and W.P.O.B., 242 f.
4. T.D., 11 ; B.W., 70. On *Mid* value, B., 1481.
5. *Matu* or " Dead one," cp. W.P.O.B., 243 f.
6. *Kús*, " cut off," M., 8566–7 ; *Lum*, crouch, squat, M., 8564.
7. This broken sign at end seems same as last sign on previous seal *Tum* " Life."

in regard to *Dax* or *Tax* and his sons, the Sanskrit Daxa (or " Daksha ") ; for in the Indian Epics " *Mīdhwas* " is recorded as a son of Daxa the grandson of Narishyanta, who was also " father " of Dama of the " Solar " race of the Mithila line [1]—a line which I find was apparently the proto-Medes or Mitani.

It is moreover of great historical significance to find the Aryan personal name of " Midas' " recorded at this early period, presumably about 2700 B.C., and on a Sumerian seal. Daxa of the Indian Epics was, as we have seen, a S'aka, *i.e.*, Saca or Geti or Goth ; and the famous Anatolian king Midas of classic Greek legend was an Aryan and presumably a Mede, and I have shown that the Medes were *Guti* or Goths.

Mīdhwas was son of Daxa, son of Citrasena,[2] the same ancestors as those of Dama of Seal VIII., Daxa being probably identical with Tax the owner of Seal VI. This Death-Amulet evidencing the death and burial of Midas' in the Indus Valley, alongside the other members of the Dax family, thus affords strong confirmation of the readings of those other seals.

There was a " Medhas," son of King Priya-vrata and brother of Dyutimat, previously mentioned, and brother to a king of Kus'a, and he adopted the religious life.[3]

The title " Seer of the Sun " is significant, and is in keeping with what we have seen of the solar religion of these seal holders. And it is to be noted that it is the *dual* Sun—*i.e.*, the Day and " Night," or returning or " Resurrecting " Sun—which is here written. This is of great interest, as this dual Sun-sign frequently occurs in Sumerian, Hitto-Phœnician and Trojan Death-Amulets, and also on the funeral Cup-marked stones of Ancient Briton monuments, as described and illustrated in my former work.[4] This conception of the Sun as of two aspects, resulted in its being placed under a pair of twin guardian Sun-angels of the Father-god (Ia, Induru or Bel), who were called by the Hittites Nāsata, the *Nāsatya*

[1] W.V.P., 3, 335.
[2] *Ib.*, 3, 335.
[3] *Ib.*, 2, 101.
[4] W.P.O.B., 247, 251, 308.

of the Vedic Aryans, frequently invoked in the Vedic hymns,[1] and by Aus'ija Kakshīvan amongst others.[2] And these twin Sun-angels are obviously the Sumerian source of the Greek myth of the inseparable twin demigods of the sky, the Dioscuri, sons of Zeus, namely, Kastor and Polydeukes. Their Fire and Water origin is evident also from the Greek myth, making them specially invoked by sailors in distress, and by their manifestation as electric fire at the mast-head of ships sailing in storms.

Seal No. XV.

Death-Amulet Seal of Uzuas' *the Seer Slave-girl of the Temple of the Sun.*

? The Vedic and Epic Us'ij, the Amorite Slave-girl priestess of Seal IV.

This Death-Amulet (Fig. 3, XV.) is of surpassing interest, as it appears to be the actual Resurrection Amulet of the Amorite Sun-priestess and "slave-girl *Us'iz*" of Seal IV., the Vedic and Epic *Us'ij*.

The inscription is also notable in that it contains a post-script at the end, in the right-hand lower corner, inserting the additional word-signs (7, 8 and 9) to complete the sense, and introduce the cherished title of "Slave-girl of the Sun." This postscript is scratched in shallow graving. And like the previous amulets this one also appears to begin its prayer for Resurrection with the invocation of the Fish of the Setting Sun, *S'ukhā*—though the upper part of this initial compound Fish-sign is broken off.

Uzu-as', as a personal name here, means in Sumerian "diviner, seer or magician" (*Uzu*) + "One or perfect" (*As'*), and thus literally "The perfect diviner." It is practically homophonous with the name of Us'ij in Seal IV.

[1] W.P.O.B., 242.

[2] R.V., 1, 116, 4, etc.

as "*Us'-iz*," *i.e.*, "The *News*(-giver) by the (divining) *Wood*"—*Us'* = "news," and *iz* = "wood." [1] And this name with the added title "Slave-girl" and the rising Sun word-

FIG. 24.—Amulet Inscription of *Uzuas'* the Seer Slave-girl of Temple of Sun.

N.B.—The postscript is placed within square brackets.

Reads: (S'u-)khā khā-as' uzu-as' matu bara [gim] gin [tum ra].
Transl.: O (Setting Sun-) Fish! The Seer *Uzuas'* the dead one of the temple [the Slave-girl] bring [to Life O Sun !]

1. Top broken off but shows below tail of Fish, and thus presumably the compound *Sú-kha* sign of previous two seals.
2. *Khā-as*, as in previous seals.
3. T.D., 400 *bis* Suppl.; B.W., 188. *Uzu*, "diviner or magician," B., 4666.
4. *Matu*, see previous seal.
5. T.D., 88; B.W., 301. *Bara* house, sanctuary, B., 6878, 6881.
6. *Gim*, see Fig. 8, Seal IV.
7. See previous seal.
8. This broken sign seems *Tum*, see previous seal.
9. T.D., 234; B.W., 337. "Rising, Sun Bright," *Ra*, M., 5741, 5747, etc.; *Ut*, *Babbar*, B., 7797, etc.

sign appears to identify her certainly with the owner of the signet Seal IV. Here it is interesting to note that the word-sign *Uzu* or "diviner" has also the synonym of *Azu*, meaning also "diviner or seer" as well as "physician"; but it will be noticed that this name is spelt on Lord

[1] See Fig. 8, Seal IV.

Mudgala's seal in Fig. 5 " *A-zu* " or " The *Water*-knower," thus implying a divination *by Water*, and not by the sacred divining *Wood-rod*. As she is styled also " The Seer or Necromancer " (*Khas'*), it is clear that Uzuas' is her personal name.

Bara, the word for " temple," literally means " house or building as well as sanctuary " ;[1] and thus incidentally discloses the Sumerian origin of this series of Aryan house words. Thus the Sanskrit *vara*, a " room " ;[2] Bengali *bari*, " house " ; Gothic Eddic *bur*, *bær*, " house " ;[3] Swedish *bur*, " house, cottage " ; English " bower," " barn " and " byre "—in which last two the sense has become degraded ; whilst the Sumerian name of this word-sign and its Akkad value *parakku*,[4] obviously survives in our word " barrack." And the Egyptian *par*, " house," is now seen to be derived from this Sumerian root, as well as the buttressed Egyptian hieroglyph for " temple," which is seen to be an adaptation of this Sumerian pictograph for " temple " or " house," as seen on this seal.

Similarly, *Ra*, " the Rising Sun," here is disclosed as the Sumerian origin of the Egyptian *Ra* ; and of the Sanskrit *Ra-vi*, " the Sun," derived from the Sanskrit *Ra*, " brightness, splendour,"[5] a word which is now seen to be derived from this Sumerian *Ra*, which secondarily meant "brightness, splendour " ;[6] and also apparently the Sumerian source of our English word " Ray."

It is highly significant in regard to this Grave-Amulet " seal " of a Sumerian Sun-priestess from the Indus Valley to find that *its prayer formula is couched in the same general form as that in the Grave-Amulet of the Aryan Amorite Sun-*

[1] B., 6876–8, presumably derived from *Bar* " wood " (or wooden *bar?*), M. 984, which implies that the early houses were made of wood bars ?

[2] M.W.D., 921. [3] V.D., 89, 92. [4] B., 6870.

[5] M.W.D., 859. Thus the ordinary Sanskrit, Hindi and Bengali name for Sun-day is still " *Ravi*-war," and the Indo-Persian for Sun-day is " *It*-war," which is presumably derived from the Sumerian synonym of this Sun sign, *Ut*.

[6] M., 5741, 5747, 5785.

priestess from Smyrna of similar or earlier date, which I have figured and deciphered and translated for the first time in my previous work. The present seal thus confirms my translation of that Amorite Grave-Amulet, and of the others, Sumerian and Trojan as well as the Cup-mark script on the tombs of the Ancient Britons.

SEAL NO. XVI.

Death-Amulet Seal of (? UKHZU) *of* (?) *Dara-saki.*

There seems to be no personal name on this seal (Fig. 3, XVI.); and the place-name appears to be " Dara-Saki " rather than Edin; and " S'aki," we have seen, was a title of the Slave-girl of Edin. The seal is especially interesting as praying for rebirth in " Heaven "—*Imin*, the " Himin " of the Eddic Goths; and for its invocation of The Sun-Hawk.

The word " Ukh-zu," if it so reads, seems to be not a personal name but an invocation to the Sun as " The Hawk " or *Ukh*—a Sumerian name which appears to be the origin of our English word " Hawk "; with the vocative second personal pronoun suffix *zu* or " thou," thus forming the invocation " O Thou (Sun-) Hawk." On the Sun-Hawk on Sumerian and Hitto-Phœnician seals and on pre-Roman Early Briton coins and monuments, and its invocation, see my former work.[1] If it be a personal name, it suggests the Gothic and Scandinavian name Hugo, Hako or Hugh.

The animal portrayed as the first part of the compound sign for the place-name is clearly by its non-bovine form, long neck and short erect tail, not an ox, but is evidently a goat or deer-antelope, the *Dar* or *Dara* of the Sumerians, thus disclosing the Sumerian origin of our English word " *Deer*." And the next two signs, we have seen, may read S'aki, thus giving a full place-name of Daras'aki or Dara-S'aki or " Dara of the S'aki land." This Dara (which may

[1] W.P.O.B., 251, 284–5; 349–50.

possibly be related to the *Daro* of the modern name Mohenjo Daro) suggests the "Darvi" and *Dars'aka* countries of the Indian Epics.[1]

Darvi was a country of the "Khattiyo" people and Kurus to the north of India.[2] And the *Dars'aka* people are

FIG. 25.—Amulet Inscription of (?) Ukhzu of (?) Dara S'aki.
Reads: Ukh-zu matu imin-bara-ga (?) dara-s'a-ki-as'.
Transl.: O Thou Sun-Hawk! the dead one bring to Heaven's house. At (?) Dara-s'aki.

1. T.D., 235; B.W., 346. *Ukh*, B., 8130.
2. T.D., 188; B.W., 7=*Zu* "thou," B., 141.
3. As before.
4. *Imin*, B., 10049. "As Heaven," W.P.O.B., 243, etc.
5. See previous Fig. and note.
6. B.W., 113, of period of Tig. Pileser, 1100 B.C. On *Dar* or *Dara*, B., 2946–7.
7. See Figs. 9, 11, etc.
8. This sign may read *Ki* or *du*.

placed next to the Gāndhāras,[3] *i.e.*, the people of the Peshwar and adjoining district of Afghanistan in the Upper Indus. And it is significant that the *Darwa* people along with the *Khas'as* are recorded as having been conquered by the Emperor Sagara,[4] who we have seen was Sargon I.

[1] W.V.P., 2, 175. [2] *Ib.*, 175. [3] *Ib.*, 174–5. [4] *Ib.*, 3, 292.

SEAL No. XVII.

Death-Amulet Seal of USSA *the Seer at Edin*
? The Vedic US'ANA.

This seal (Fig. 3, XVII.) is important as invoking the One God as "The All-Perfect One," *S'ar* [1]—by the word-sign of the Great Circle (the Greek *Saros*) of the Cup-mark script, which in cuneiform is written in "diamond" or lozenge shape as here. This is a usual title of the Father-

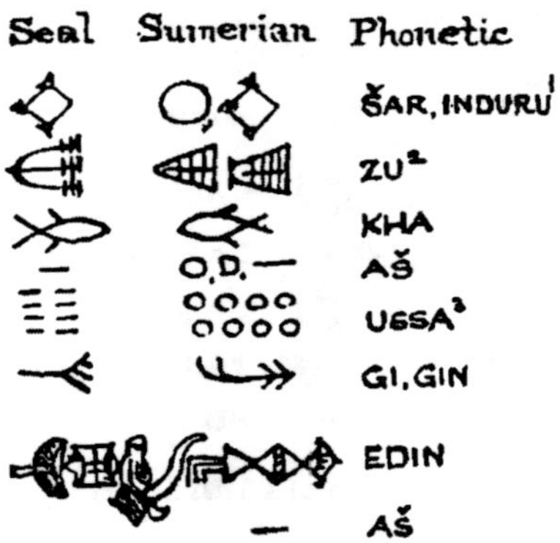

FIG. 26.—Amulet Inscription of *Ussa* the Seer of Edin.

Reads: S'ar-zu kha-as' ussa gin [tum] edin-as'.
Transl.: O Thou All-perfect God! the Seer *Ussa* bring [to Life] at Edin.

1. T.D., 206 and 476; B.W., 353. *S'ar*, B., 8208 and W.P.O.B., 242, 244 f.
2. T.D., 186; B.W., 6, and see previous seal.
3. B.W., 437, pl. 171.

god Induru (or "E-a" or Indra),[2] on amulets and Cup-marked inscriptions, as I have shown in my former work.[3] And incidentally its second sign *zu*, "thou," confirms the reading of this sign in the previous seal, where it is also the second sign.

Us'anā, also named Us'anas' Kavya, was an ancient Vedic

[1] B., 8272. [2] W.P.O.B., 241 f., 323 f. [3] *Ib.*, 237 f.

seer mentioned in many hymns, who worshipped Indra;[1] and he is associated in one of these hymns with Aus'ija Kakshīvan (of Seal I.) as an Indra worshipper.[2]

SEAL NO. XVIII.

Death-Amulet Seal of S'ABTAR *of Edin.*

This seal (Fig. 3, XVIII.) appears to be the Death-Amulet of the owner of the signet Seal XII., whose name seems to equate with that of the Epic teacher Savitri.

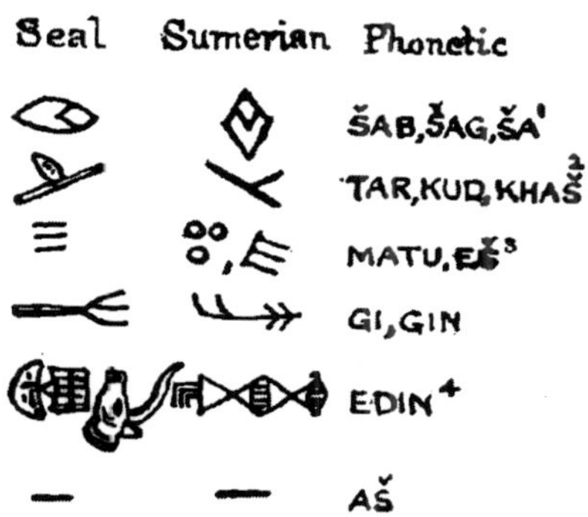

FIG. 27.—Amulet Inscription of *S'abtar* of Edin.

Reads: S'ab-tar matu gin [tum] edin-as'.
Transl.: *S'abtar,* the dead one, bring [to Life] at Edin.

1. T.D., 255; B.W., 340. *S'ab, S'a, Sag,* B., 7988.
2. T.D., 123; B.W., 12. *Tar, Kud,* B., 373, etc.; M., 290, 303, 316; *Khas'*, B., 328.
3. *Matu* as before.
4. As before.

SEAL NO. XIX.

Death-Amulet Seal of Gurgu.

This seal (Fig. 3, XIX.), the last of the series, seems the Amulet of Gurgu, probably the Vedic *Garga,* a priest of Divo-Dāsa or King Tarṣi. It also invokes the Resurrecting

[1] R.V., 1, 51, 10; 83, 5; 121, 12; 4, 162, etc. [2] *Ib.*, 1, 51, 10–13.

Sun-Fish like the majority of those other death-amulets; and seeks resurrection in Heaven.

Garga, surnamed Bhārad-vāja, or "The strength of the Bharads (Bharats)," was a Vedic seer and reputed author of a hymn to Indra [1] in praise of the bounty he received from Divo-Dāsa, *i.e.*, King Tarsi, great-grandson of Uruas' ("Ur-Ninā"), which places him about 3020 B.C. He significantly calls Indra in one verse by the title of *S'akra* [2] —that is, the *Sakko* of the Pali and a favourite title used by

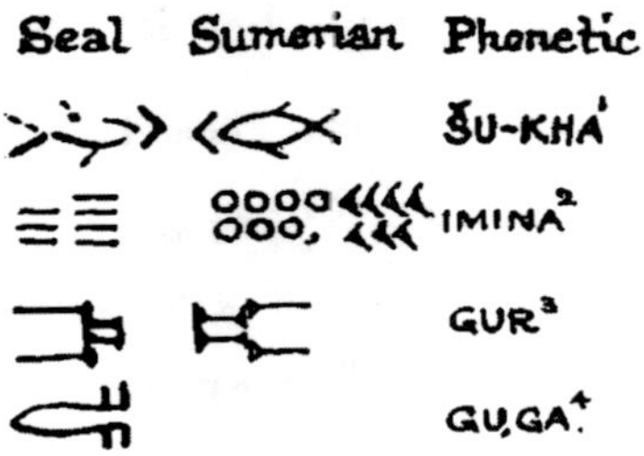

FIG. 28.—Amulet Inscription.

Reads: S'u-khā imin gur-gu.
Transl.: O Setting Sun-Fish to Heaven Gur-gu (bring)!

1. and 2. As before.
3. T.D., 60; B.W., 187. *Gur*, B., 4654.
4. As before.

Buddha for Indra. This Indra-name, I find, is clearly derived from the Sumerian title of *Sakh* for the Father-god Induru as "The enthroned Lord"—a word which is disguised by Assyriologists as "Enlil" or "Enki."

There are a few other later Epic priests and princes of the name of Garga less known.[2] This Sumerian name Gurgu seems probably the source of the Greco-Median "Gorgias" and the English "George."

[1] R.V., 6, 47. He seems identical with the Epic Garga, a descendant of King Bharat, and bearing the synonym *Brihat*, *i.e.* "Brit-on," cp. W.P., 4, 137.

[2] *Ib.*, 6, 47, 11.

IX

Personal, Tribal and Clan Names and Titles on Seals III. to XIX.

Disclosing names of famous Vedic and Epic priests, kings, queens and princes, Sargon I. of Agade, Su'sin of Ur, etc.; and tribal or clan names A-Mer (Amorite), Ari and Har[-ri] (Aryan), Gad or Kad (Phœnician), Guti (Goth), Kaz (Kassi), Khaiti (Catti or Hitt-ite) and Saki (Sacæ, Scyth and Sax-on).

The personal names and titles of "*As's'ias'* the *Barugu* seer" (the Vedic seer Aus'ija the B'rigu) and "*Kan(-wa)* the *Barama*" (or Kanwa the Brahman) of Seals I. and II. have already been discussed in Chap. VI.

The other personal names inscribed on Seals III. to XIX. comprise the following Vedic and Epic priests, kings, queens and heroes, the Sanskrit form of whose name is placed within brackets: another *Kan-we* (Kanwa), the A-Mer Slave-girl Us'iz of *Uriki* (the Us'ij Slave-girl Wricayā, wife of Aus'ija), *S'us'ena*, prince of Gus'a (Sushena the Kus'ika, or King S'usin or S'uas'enzu of Ur Dynasty), *Tax*, the minister of *Sirgana* or *Sagunu* of *Agdu* (Daxa or Daksha re S'akuni as Sargon I.), *Sagara* of *Agdu* (King Sagara of Ayodhya), *Damu* the Guti son of *Dax* (Dama "son" of Daxa the S'āka), As's'ias' the Kaz of Gus'i (Aus'iji the Kās'i), *Kan(-wa) S'ar* . . . (Kanwa S'rayasa ?), *Gal-'ha Bargu* (Gālawa B'rigu), *S'abtar* (Savitri ?); and on the Grave-Amulets *Ukgu* the *Gad, Midas'* (Mīdhwas "son" of Daxa), *Uzuas'* the Diviner

Slave-girl of Sun-temple (Us'ij, slave-girl wife of Aus'ija), *Ussa* the seer of Edin and *Gurgu* (Garga the B'arat). Amongst these personal names the Aryan "*Midas'*" is noteworthy at this early period.

The tribal clan or racial titles found on the seals comprise the following:

Ari and *Har* on Seals IV. and VIII., etc., as "Arya-n," see notes on these seals and in my former work.[1]

Gad or *Kad* on Seals XI. and XIII. is a title of Phœnicians, with Sanskrit equivalent *Cedi*, see my previous work for details.[2] The form *Khād* is used by Uruas' or Ur-Ninā, see Chap. V. and Appendix I.

Guti or *Goth* on Seal VII., see details in my previous work.[3]

Kaz is obviously a contraction of "*Kazzi*," a recognized form of spelling Kas's'i, the dynastic clan title of the Kassi or Cassites of Babylonia. In the form *Kās'i* it was a clan title of the early Panch-āla or Sumero-Phœnician kings in the Indian Epics; and Dīrgha-tamas, the forefather of Aus'ija, was of this line,[4] therefore Aus'ija Kakshīvan and his descendants, the Gotamas, were Kās'i. "*Kazzi*" is the form of "Kassi" or "Cassi," which is used by the Phœnician-Briton king Partolon on his monument of about 400 B.C. in Scotland.[5] On this *Kas* and *Cas* and *Cassi* title of ancient Brito-Phœnician kings who also stamped it on their coins, see my former work, where the origin of this "Kazzi" and the "Kassi" title is disclosed in detail.[6]

Khaiti seems used for Khati, Khatti, Catti or "Hitt-ite," the Khattiyo of Pali and Khattri of Hindi as seen in next chapter. And Alexander the Great found the *Kathai*-oi tribe, noted for its handsome appearance and their country

1 W.P.O.B., 257 f., 412 f.
2 *Ib.*, 18, 74 f., 168, 180, 200, 262.
3 *Ib.*, 170, 331.
4 W.V.P., 4, 32.
5 *Ib.*, 32, 211.
6 *Ib.*, 47 f., 202 f., 211, 274 f.

Kathai-ai, hereabouts between Mohenjo Daro and Harappa, on the Lower Ravi and Sutlej tributaries of the Indus.[1]

Saki is used in a tribal as well as territorial sense, and seems the Sumerian source of the *S'aka* or *S'akya* tribe of Ancient India, the *Sacæ* of the Greco-Romans for the Scyths, and of the name " Sax-on."

[1] Arrian ; V.N., 88 ; Strabo, 699.

X

Place-names on the Indus Valley Seals and their Identification

Disclosing " Edin " as Sumerian city-state on Indus, with capital " Khaitisiga " at Mohenjo Daro as " City of the Hittites " ; and " Saki-Land " as " S'āka-Land " of the Maga (or Magi) Sun-worshippers.

We now discover the location and identity in the Indus Valley of the chief place-names in the seals : " Edin " and " Khaiti-siga " and " Saki."

" *Edin*," the place-name most frequently recorded in these seals, we have already found recorded in the documents of the Early Sumerians and in the identical monogram as in these seals, as detailed in Chap. V. There we have seen that the Sumero-Phœnician king Uruas' (the Haryas'wa of the Vedas and Indian Epics, the so-called " Ur-Ninā " of Assyriologists) of S'irlapur on the Persian Gulf about 3100 B.C., claimed to have " built," or " caused to be built," two Edins as " Forts of the House of the Sun-god." One of these was " Gu-Edin " in the Mesopotamian delta, a few miles to the north-west of his seaport capital of S'irlapur, and it continued to be regarded as so sacred that his grandson restored it, and Gudia (Gadhi of the Indian Epics and the " Gudea " of Assyriologists) about 2400 B.C. in one of his official documents confirmed its freedom from the payment of taxes,[1] thus showing that it was a shrine, and not the name of the province of S'irlapur or Lagash as usually supposed.

[1] R.B.H., 77 f. ; K.H.S., 271.

The other *Edin* or "*Edin*" proper, the site of which has hitherto been unknown, we then found was a distant tributary state of King Uruas', under the governorship of his eldest son and successor, its "capturer," Lord (A-)Mad-gal, the Mudgala of the Vedas and Epics. We further found that this Edin was described by the Sumerians as "The captured Land of Edin," wherein the word for "Land" is spelt by the word-sign *Sakh*, which possibly connoted the "S'āka-Land" (or Land of the Sacæ, Getæ, or Goths) of the Indian Epics, and the especial seat of the *Maga* (or Magi) Sun-worshippers in the Indus Valley.

We further found that this outlandish Edin was also called by the Sumerians "The Land (or city) of *Saki* of the temple (or house) of The Slave-girl," and was also defined as "Land (or city) of the Priest-queen of Bel." And we found that two of the seals on decipherment proved to be actually inscribed as those of "The Slave-girl" (Seals IV. and XV.).

We still further found the positive evidence on Seal III., that the owner of that signet appears to call his city in the Indus Valley "The *Second* (Edin)." All this cumulative evidence established the identity of this land of "Edin" of the Sumero-Phœnician king Uruas' with this "Edin" of the seals in the Indus Valley—the name "Edin" being applied to that city-state presumably from the Edin temple of the Sun at its capital.

In Indian traditional literature the only country or place-name resembling "Edin" is "*Udyāna*," the ancient name for the state of Swat *in a valley of the Upper Indus*[1] (see map, p. 7) and famous for its fine Indo-Scythian Buddhist sculptures,[2] as the traditional homeland of King Sibi, son of

[1] B.H.T., I, 119 f. In Indian Epic tradition it seems confused with Ujjain.
[2] See my Report on Mission for collecting Indo-Scythic Sculptures, Beng. Govt. Press, 1895; and in *Trans. Internat. Orient. Cong.*, Paris, 1897, sec. I, 245 f., which disclosed the *Gothic* arch there in sculptures of second to third centuries A.D., *i.e.*, about a thousand years before its supposed origin.

Usinara, and his "Sibi" people.[1] The name possibly also appears in "Udayana" and "Udāyin" (or "Of *Udyan*"), titles of several princes in the Indian Epics, and in the Vedic "Audanya" or "Of *Odana*," the epithet of a priest or layman named Mundibha.[2] And there is an Ayodhin on the Sutlej below Ferozepore, *i.e.*, more or less opposite Harappa (see map).[3]

The name "Edin," which is also spelt "Etin" in Sumerian,[4] *is however fortunately preserved and definitely located in the Lower Indus Valley as* "OTIN" *by the Buddhist pilgrim Hiuen Tsiang.* This remarkably accurate geographer in his pilgrimages to the chief Buddhist shrines throughout India at the beginning of the seventh century A.D., is our chief authority for the geographical topography of Ancient India. He records the distances along the roads in Chinese *li*, of which at that period about seven go to the English mile. The province of Sind (his "Sintu") at that period was restricted to a tract in the middle Indus Valley, between Multan and the modern Sukker (see map, p. 7); but he places Otin (*i.e.*, Edin) "under the protection of Sind."

Starting with our extracts from his narrative from Multan as a fixed point (see map, p. 7), he says:

"From this (Multan) going north-east 700 li (*i.e.*, about 100 miles) we come to the country of *Po-fa-to* (*Parvata ?*). . . . Here are four *stupas* built by King Asoka."[5] Here it is to be noted the Asoka *stupas* here referred to are almost certainly those at Harappa, the excavation of which has yielded several of these seals; as Harappa is approximately in the direction and distance from Multan thus indicated, and there are no other Asoka stupas known in this area.

He then continues, after describing that country:

"Leaving the Sintu country (? Parvata or Harappa ?) and going south-west 1500 or 1600 li (about 215 or 230 miles) we come to the kingdom of O-TIN-*po-chi-lo*.[6] The

[1] B.H.T., 1, 125, and cp. W.V.P., 4, 121 f.
[2] V.N., 88.
[3] M.K.I., 1, 126.
[4] B., 4521.
[5] B.H.T., 2, 275.
[6] Also spelt by him "*O-tien*."

country is about 5000 li in circuit. The chief town is called *Khie-tsi-shi-fa-lo*, and is about 30 li round. *It*[1] *lies on the River Sin-tu and borders the ocean. . . . It is under the protection of Sin-tu. . . .* King Asoka built stupas on the spots consecrated by the sacred traces, six in number. Going west from this, less than 2000 li, we come to the country of *Long-kie-lo* . . . it borders on the ocean. It is on the route to the kingdom of the Western women (the Amazonian matriarchists of Van of Semiramis). . . . From this going north-west we come to the kingdom of *Po-la-see* (PERSIA)."[2]

Now this capital on the River Indus of the kingdom of OTIN-*pochilo*, under the protection of Sind, and bordering the ocean, is seen by its relative position and distance from Multan, on the one hand, and Persia and the Indian Ocean on the other, to *correspond clearly to the location of the Buddhist ruins at Mohenjo Daro*, where most of the "*Edin*" seals were unearthed, and implies that this "*Otin*" is identical with the Sumerian "Edin" or "Etin." And from the occurrence of seals with the name "Edin" at Harappa (*e.g.*, Seal I.), and the occurrence of the name "Uḍyāna" for the Upper Indus district of Swat, it would appear probable that the whole of the Indus Valley from Edin city upwards was known in ancient times as "The Land of *Edin*."

The second part of this country name "*Pochilo*," as spelt by the Chinese, is apparently the equivalent of the modern "*Bukkur*" or "*Behker*"—*r* being absent in Chinese and replaced by *l*. "Bukkur," the "Behker" or "Bhaker" of the older maps of Rennell and Vincent, is the name of the ancient town and district on the east bank of the Indus opposite Sukkur, and about forty miles to the north-east of Mohenjo Daro (see map). Behker was a very ancient prehistoric settlement, for neolithic implements and cores were

[1] The kingdom of Otin.

[2] B.H.T., 2, 276–7.

found here,[1] as at Mohenjo Daro. At the pilgrims' visit this district was thus joined to Otin (Edin) forming the "Otin-Pochiro" state.

The name of the capital town of "*Otin*" country as preserved by Hiuen Tsiang, namely, *Khie-tsi-shi-fa-lo*, well equates with *Khaitt-sig* of Seal III., with the addition of *pura* or "city." This name suggests that it may possibly mean "The Lower city of the Khatti"; and Seal IX. appears to give the reading "Fort *Sig*," *i.e.*, "Lower Fort."

This meaning of "Lower city of the *Khatti*" or "Hittites" for this old Sumerian city-capital and port of the Indus Valley—wherein *Khatti* is the "Khattiyo" of the Pali, "Khattri" of Hindi, and the "Catti" title of the Ancient Britons on their coins, etc.[2]—receives support from the facts: Firstly, that the handsome *Kathai* tribe were located in its neighbourhood at Alexander's visit; secondly, that it was hereabouts, at Sukker, I was led by quite independent evidence to fix the crossing of the Indus by the "Great Indo-Aryan Invasion" of Khattiyo Syria-Phœnicians (*Kuru-Panch*-āla) in their exodus from Syria-Phœnicia via Persia to Hindustan or the Ganges Valley about 700 B.C., when I completed my *Origin of the Indo-Aryans and their Civilization* over ten years ago; and thirdly, that the Indus Valley retained the name "*Hiti*," *i.e.*, "Hitt-ite" on its coins down to about the seventh century A.D.

The name "*Hiti*" is recognized by Assyriologists as a common late dialectic form of *Khati* or *Khatti*, in which the initial hard *K* has dropped out; and this "*Hit*" is the form adopted by the Jews in their Old Testament for these Aryan or Amorite people, which our English translators have romanized into "*Hitt*-ite." The Khatti or Hitt-ite people themselves sometimes spelt the name "Kha-it-ti," which equates with the seal. Now a fine

[1] B. Foote, *Ind. Prehist. Antiquities*, Madras, 1916, 158.
[2] W.P.O.B., 6, etc., etc.

gold coin *bearing undeciphered Hittite hieroglyphs* is figured by Sir A. Cunningham of the Indian Archæological Survey,[1] as being probably found in Sind or Multan; and is conjecturally dated to about the seventh century A.D. or earlier.[2] It contains the portrait of a king of fine Aryan *Gothic* type, with the legend: HITI-*vi ca Airān ca parames'wara, i.e.,* "Paramount Lord of *Hiti*-land and of Airan (or Eastern Persia)." This "Land of the Hiti" has been conjectured to be "the Panjab,"[2] presumably because Mooltan is now detached from Sind and been allocated to that Upper Indus province.

Another reference to *Hiti*, presumably as title of the ancient Indus Valley state, is found in the list of *Parāda* kings of Western India—wherein Parāda appears to be the Parthian form of Barata, B'arata, or Brihad or "Brit-on." One of these kings is styled *S'ri* HITI-*vira Airana ka Pāradeswara, S'ri Vāhiti-Gana Deva-Ganita,*[3] *i.e.,* "The worshipful *Hiti* hero of Airana, Lord of the *Pārada* (Parthians or Barats), the worshipful Vāhiti-Gana Deva-Ganita." This appears to establish the use of *Hiti*, a dialectic form of Khaiti or "Hittite" for ancient Sind; and the survival of the old personal Sumerian name of the seals, Gana (or Kana), is noteworthy.

"*S'āka*-Land, or Land of the Sacæ, Scyths, Getæ or Goths,"[4] was also an ancient name for the Indus Valley in the Indian Epics, and obviously the "*Saki*-Land of Edin" of the Sumerians as above noted. We have seen that the Vedic hymn of Aus'ija of Seal I. records that his patron king "on the banks of the Indus" was "the son of Bhavya." And the Indian Epics tell us that Bhavya, son of Priya-Vrata, "was appointed to reign over S'āka-land";[5] and

[1] A.S.I., v. 123. Also fig. in *Numismat. Chr.*, 1894, pl. xii (x) 9, p. 291.
[2] Rapson, *Coins of India*, 1898, 31.
[3] C. Lassen, *Indische Altertums-kunde*, 1847, I, 9.
[4] On the interchange of these ethnic names, see W.P.O.B., 331 f.
[5] W.V.P., 2, 101.

that " the sons of Bhavya king of S'āka-land " were the rulers over that land with its *seven* rivers.[1]

This " S'āka " title for the Indus Valley is probably " The S'AKH *Land " mentioned by the son of Lord Mudgala,* King Bi(d)as'nadi (" Eannatum ") in his edict on the " State of the Vultures " as conquered by him. And he mentions it after Elam.[2] The name " Saca-stene " or " Land of the Sacas " was restricted by the Greco-Romans to the south-western part of their province of Ariana in Persia, and called " Saka-stan " by the Persians, the modern Seistan (see map, p. 32).

This S'āka-land of the Indus Valley, now identified with the *Saki*-land of Edin of the seals, was the land of the *Maga* (or Magi) Sun-worshippers,[3] who now would seem to be the descendants of the Sun-worshipping Sumerians of the seals, or of a later wave of the same people.

The most famous Sun-temple hitherto known in the whole of India, and presumably a branch of the Edin one, was still flourishing in this region in the seventh century A.D. at Mooltan, between Mohenjo Daro and Harappa; and it was also an oracle with vestal virgins like the Sumerian " Ninā " Sun-temple of Uruas' at Lagash and of Us'iz at Edin. It is therefore of especial interest and importance to read the Chinese pilgrim's description of it at that period, all the more so as it illustrates the humane simple fire and flower offerings of the Sumerian Sun-worshippers of the beneficent Father-god, as opposed to the bloody sacrifices of the aboriginal Moon and Mother cult, so abhorrent to the Sun-worshippers. And like those of the Early Sumerians it had a hospital attached to it.

Hiuen Tsiang, whose descriptions of the sites and monuments of Ancient India I have found so trustworthy in my explorations and excavations at Pataliputra (Patna), Udyana (Swat), Kapilavastu, etc., as others also have found them

[1] W.V.P., 2, 198. [2] Cp. R.B., 91 and T.D.I., 37. [3] W.V.P., 2, 381 f.

elsewhere, writes: "There is (at Multan) a temple dedicated to the Sun, very magnificent and profusely decorated. The image of the Sun-god is cast in yellow gold and ornamented with rare gems. Its divine insight is mysteriously manifested. Women play their music, light their torches, offer their flowers and perfumes to honour it. *This custom has been continued from the very first.* The kings and high families of the five Indies never fail to make their offerings of gems and precious stones. They have founded a house of mercy, in which they provide food and drink and medicines for the poor and sick, affording succour and sustenance. Men from all countries come here to offer up their prayers. There are always some thousands doing so. On the four sides of the temple are tanks with flowering groves where one can wander about without restraint."[1] This old Sun-temple disappears along with the equally benign Indian Buddhism at the destructive Mohammedan invasion by fanatical iconoclasts, and the rise of modern Brahmanism with its incorporation of matriarchist rites of wholesale sanguinary sacrifices to demons.

The place-names "*Uri*," "*Uriki*" and "*Agdu*" of the seals have already been discussed under Seals IV., V., and VI. and their foot-notes. "*Uri-ki*" or "City (or land) of *Uri*" literally means "City (or land) of the Akkads or Amorites."[2] It may denote the city of Ur, or of "Uruki," *i.e.*, Erech the modern Warka.

"*Gus'a* or *Gus'i* Land" of Seals V., VIII. and X. appears to represent the "*Kus'a* Land" of the Indian Epics. "*Kus'a* Land" is always referred to in the Epics as a country distinct from S'aka-Land, and was possibly an ancient name for Mesopotamia.[3]

"*Ag-du*," if it does occur, would seem a dialectic form

[1] B.H.T., 2, 274.

[2] Cp. B.W., 316.

[3] On Kus'a country, see W.V.P., 2, 101, 109, 129 f.; on dynasty, *Ib.*, 4, 26 f., 138 f. The former glories of King Kusa and of his city Kusā-wati are repeatedly referred to by Buddha the S'akya. C.J.T., 1, 231; 5, 141 f.

of spelling " Agadu " (or " Agade "), the usual form of the name of Sargon's capital. His city-name, however, also reads, I find, *A-zu-tu* in his autobiography discovered by General Rawlinson ; [1] and thus equates fairly with the Indian " Ajodhya " or " Ayodhya " capital of Sargon I., under his solar title of " Sagara."

" *Harappa*," on the Rāvi, appears to me to be probably the Vedic *Hariyūpīyā* on the " *Yavyā* " River, where a king called " Cāyamāna son of Diva-vrata " (? Cyawana son of Divo-Dāsa) [2] and of the Pārthu clan (Parthian or Barat), along with " three thousand mailed warriors " defeated the Wricīs under Waras'ika, through the aid of Indra.[3] It thus becomes a question whether this *Wrici* tribal title may be related to the " Wricaya " or " Uri-ki " title of " the slave-girl Usij," and thus explain the story of her being a " captive " or " slave " of the Sumerians at Edin, presumably on their capture of Harappa as an up-country port on the route to the gold-fields of Tibet, in the reign of the son of Divo-Dāsa or King Tarsi, the great-grandson of Uruas', about 3020–3000 B.C.

Regarding the name " *Mohenjo Daro*," we have seen that the second part of that name, " Daro," appears to represent the older form of the Indo-Persian word *Darya* " the sea," derived as I have shown from the Sumerian *Duru* " the sea or water " and the source of the Cymric *Dwr* " water," etc., especially as we find this name Darya along the course of the Indus, even above Sukker, for the depressed areas representing former lakes. As regards the first part of the name, " Mohenjo," in view of the prominence given to the Buffalo

[1] C.T. : C.I.W.A., 3 pl. 4, No. 47. The name usually read " Azupiranu," reads, I find, A-zu-tu rax-a-ni or " The destroyed *Azutu* " (cp. on *raxani*, M.D., 957). Sargon uses that phrase in describing this ancestral city at his birth ; and I find that he was the son of a Sumerian king who was killed and his capital destroyed by a rival, and that Sargon was a posthumous son, who afterwards recovered his patrimony and rebuilt the capital as " Agadu." This now explains the references in his birth-story which have remained a puzzle to Assyriologists.

[2] See Appendix IV.

[3] R.V., 6, 27.

on the seals of Edin, I think it is possible that "Mohenjo" may be a dialectic form of the still current name of "Mains" or "Mang" for a buffalo,[1] which is a nasalized form of the Sanskrit "*Mahisha*"—a name now disclosed to be derived from the Sumerian *Ma-a-su*, "cattle," and especially "wild cattle."[2] Thus, "Mohenjo-Daro" would mean "The Lagoon of the Wild Buffaloes"; and we have seen that the Wild Buffalo was evidently indigenous there.

[1] In Bengal and Bihar where wild buffalo still exist, B.M., 491. The more common name *Bains* is thus seen to be a corruption of "Mains," *M* and *B* being freely interchangeable, thus "Mombay" for "Bombay."

[2] Br., 1749 and M.D., 155.

XI

Date of Indo-Sumerian Seals

PALÆOGRAPHICALLY, we have seen that the archaic form of the Sumerian writing on the seals suggests for some of them the remote date of "about 4000 B.C." to about 3000 B.C., whilst others betray certain conventional modifications of the Sumerian script which only came into vogue in the time of Sargon I. (about 2800 B.C.), and of Gudia (about 2400 B.C.), and of the Ur Dynasty (about 2300 B.C.).

The positive evidence, on the other hand, from the decipherment of the inscriptions on the seals, while generally confirming these inferences of palæography, by disclosing some of the authors as historical Mesopotamian princes of approximately fixed dates, and as Vedic sages and priestesses of relatively fixed position in the Indian Epic King-lists which now can be dated, as I have shown, through the Mesopotamian King-lists, it at the same time lowers the extreme date for the oldest of these seals to about 3100 B.C. For it is known that the Sumerians and their successors continued to use archaic script as *seal* characters, for sacred or amulet or magical purposes, in later times long after the current contemporary script had acquired a less archaic form. This is evidenced by the seals impressed as attestations upon clay-tablets of relatively later dates, just as some people nowadays use Runic and "Old English" letters and "Gnostic characters" on their signets.

The rudest, and thus presumably the oldest of these seals, No. X., namely, "Kan(-we) S'ar . . .," may yet be dated about 3100 B.C., that is the approximate date for the

Emperor Uruas'-the-Khad (or "Phœnician," or "Ur-Ninā "), who we found " built or caused to be built " Edin, " in a captured land," which has proved by the new evidence to be this Indus Valley, captured by his son Mudgala.

Thus the seals of the Vedic priest As's'ias' (Aus'ija, Seal I.) and the seals of the slave-girl Usiz and Uzuas' (IV. and XV.) as well as the Kanwa priests (II., III.) appear to date to about this epoch. King Sagara's seal (VII.) along with the seal of "Tax the minister of Sirgana or Saguna" (No. VI.) can be placed with comparative certainty about 2750 B.C., within the reign of Sargon I. of Agade; and similarly, or soon after, the seal of "Damu son of Dax" (VII.).

The seal of "Prince S'us'ēna" (No. V.) absolutely identifies him with S'usin or S'uas'sin "son" and successor of Buras'-sin (Bur-Sin I.) of the Ur Dynasty about 2350 B.C. And this seal appears to be one of the last of the series.

XII

Historical Results and Effects of Discoveries

THE historical effects of these decipherments of this large series of Sumerian seals from the Indus Valley are of far-reaching importance. In recovering one of the earliest, if not the earliest, lost chapters of the History of Indian Civilization, and also lost chapters in the History of the Early Sumerians and Phœnicians in Mesopotamia, in regard to their race, the rise of three dynasties, and their early seafaring, commercial and colonizing activities, and the manner in which they spread the Aryan Civilization over the Ancient World, they shift the currently accepted racial pivots of the history of the World's "Higher Civilization" by establishing still more firmly my discovery that the Sumerians and Phœnicians were racially Aryans.

The decipherment of this large series of Sumerian seals from the Indus Valley, dating from about 3100 B.C. to 2300 B.C., whilst fully confirming and further establishing my discovery that *the "Sumerians" were the Early Aryans*, the early heroes of the Vedas, and the authors of Indian Civilization; it also confirms and further establishes my discovery that *the leading dynasty of Early Sumerians on the Persian Gulf from about* 3100 B.C. *onwards were Phœnicians, and that the Phœnicians properly so-called were Aryans in race and speech, and were the leading pioneers of Aryan Civilization over the world; and that in particular the introducers of Aryan Civilization into Ancient India were mainly the Aryan Phœnicians.*

The names and personalities of the chief leaders of the

Early Aryan merchants, who from their seaport on the Persian Gulf first exploited the economic and commercial resources of the Indus Valley from 3100 B.C. onwards, are now recovered from their actual personal signets and seals, as well as the names of the well-known Vedic Sun-worshipping priests and priestesses who accompanied them and settled and died there.

We discover that the enterprising seafaring Aryan Sumerian emperor who founded the Indus colony was the founder of the First Phœnician Dynasty about 3100 B.C.; and that he was the son of the famous Hercules of the Phœnicians, who is now conclusively identified with the Sumerian hero "Gilgamesh" (or "The Fire-priest") of Erech and disclosed for the first time as a historical Aryan king of fixed date about 3150 B.C., as detailed in Appendix V.

The first expedition of these Phœnician mariner traders who formed the first settlement on the Indus, is disclosed to have been under the leadership of the merchant-prince Lord Madgal (Mudgala of the Vedas and Indian Epics), the eldest son and successor of the Sumerian emperor of Mesopotamia, Uruas'-the-Khad (or Phœnician), the King Hary-as'wa of the Vedas and Epics, with his capital on the Persian Gulf. And this fact incidentally confirms the truth of the tradition reported by Herodotus that the Phœnicians were settled on the Persian Gulf *before* 2800 B.C., when they first established Tyre on the Mediterranean. And we now recover a wonderful lost chapter on the manner in which the Early Phœnicians pursued their trade along the Persian Gulf to the Arabian Sea and Indus Valley and penetrated and colonized the latter for about eight centuries from 3100 B.C. onwards in their exploitation of its mineral and other wealth.

This first settlement and colonization of the Indus Valley by these Aryan Phœnicians is proved by the record of Uruas' in regard to his having "built" Edin; and by the seal of Lord Mudgala as "the capturer" and "minister" there, holding the Edin state as a "captured" colony of the Sumerian empire of Mesopotamia. It seems to be the "S′akh-land" held by King Mudgala's son. It was also, we found, a colony of that empire in the time of Sargon I. (2800 B.C.). The "Magan" tributary land of Gudia (2450 B.C.) was possibly, we have seen, within it, and some of the seals are of Gudia's period. It was still a colony of that empire in the time of S′us′in, the second last king of the Ur Dynasty (about 2350–2300 B.C.). And it appears to have remained throughout a mere colony of that empire; as no local title of "king" is found on any of the seals—the Vedic reference to Bhavya and his son the patron of Aus′ija Kakshīvan as "unconquered king of Sindhu" may have been merely a bardic compliment, though it is of course possible that local kings may have set themselves up in the intervals of imperial weakness, as they did in that other dependency of Mesopotamia, Sus′a. Nor is there any evidence that the Indus Valley was a colony of an ancient independent Sus′a (or Elam). At the same time we gain an insight into the reality of the claim proudly inscribed by these ancient Sumerian emperors on their monuments in Mesopotamia, to be "King of the Four Quarters of the World," "Lord of the Lower Sea (Persian Gulf and Arabian Sea or Indian Ocean) and of the Upper Sea of the Setting Sun (Mediterranean)."

The sudden cessation of the seals with the end of the Ur Dynasty, about 2300 B.C., suggests that the Isin Dynasty—a dynasty now called "Amorite" [1]—which overthrew the Ur line, lost the sovereignty over the Indus Valley. And this in association with the massacre by Bur-as′ Sin I. (Paras′u) of "the sons of Hary-as′wa," *i.e.*, of the Phœnician princes of the line of Uruas′-the-Khad, appears to have meant the loss of the Indus Valley by these Early Phœnicians. It is

[1] C.E.A., 90–1.

possible however, and even probable, that further excavation of the Indus Valley sites may unearth other and later series of Sumerian or cuneiform seals or tablets, of later rulers there.

The strategical position of Mohenjo Daro on an island in the Lower Indus near what had been its old delta, and of Harappa on one of the main confluences of the Upper Indus, implies that these Early Sumero-Phœnician merchant-princes held the water-way up the Indus Valley and the lines of communications with the gold-fields of Tibet. On the other hand, it is noteworthy that so far there is no evidence yet forthcoming that this early wave of Sumero-Phœnicians penetrated to and settled in the Ganges Valley, the Brahmanist traditional centre of Indo-Aryan Civilization and the seat of the so-called " Aryan Invasion of India " of modern Indianists—an invasion which I have been led by a series of facts, before mentioned, to ascribe to a much later branch of Syrio-Phœnicians introducing a later form of the same Sumerian civilization and religion, and at a no earlier date than about 700 B.C.

The civilization disclosed by the seals and their language and religion and the cultural objects and buildings associated with them *is purely Sumerian as found in Mesopotamia*, and is not of independent local origin in the Indus Valley. And in keeping with this exotic source, we find the civilization suddenly appears there as a fully-fledged Higher Civilization of the Sumerian type of that period.

The cultural and religious objects found associated with these seals are of the Sumerian and Hitto-Phœnician type. The necklaces are generally of the Sumerian and Hitto-Phœnician pattern; and necklaces we have seen are mentioned as treasures in the Vedic hymn by the author of Seal I., resident on the Indus. The crude terra-cotta figurines of birds generally resemble those of the early Hittites,[1] and similarly the animal-head figurines,[2] which were favourite

[1] C.M.C., pl. 18, 1617. [2] *Ib.*, pl. 16, 5; 17, 3, 9, etc.; 18, 7, 8, etc.

nursery toys and buried with children. The crude horned headdress of the female figurine is obviously a crude representation of the horned headdress of the Hitto-Sumerian ladies seen on their seals.[1] Similarly, the painted ware is like the Hittite.[2] Glazed tiles were a speciality of the Phœnicians and Early Sumerians, and marble flags and house-drains are found in early Phœnician buildings at Crete, etc., and at Hittite Carchemish, where also are masonry and brick graves within the side walls of houses[3] as at Mohenjo Daro. The votive stone-maces are of the Hitto-Sumerian pattern, and as seen on the Edin seal of Lord Mudgala (Fig. 5, p. 35); and amongst those found in the excavations there may possibly be the actual originals of the sacred pair used by Mudgala in his famous exploit at Edin, and figured on that seal.

The art displayed on these seals is of a very advanced type, implying long familiarity and proficiency in the naturalistic drawing of animals, and of engraving on a minute scale on jewels and hard stones, with an artistic ability and standard far beyond anything found in Anglo-Saxon England.

The religion expressed on these seals also reflects the purer monotheism of the Early Sumerians over a millennium of years before the birth of Abraham, as opposed to the polytheism hitherto arbitrarily ascribed to them by Assyriologists, from Prof. Sayce downwards, with the supposititious female god "Ninā."[4] We now see the original documentary evidences for the belief of these Early Aryan Sumero-Phœnicians in the One Father-God of Heaven and his Sun-angel and in the Resurrection from the Dead, in the pathetic prayers for that Resurrection which are engraved on their Death-Amulets. There is also disclosed the Sumerian origin of the "Sun-worship," which still survives widely in modern

[1] See W.P.O.B., Fig. 35, etc.
[2] C.M.C., pl. 3, 10–14.
[3] B.M.C. ii., 39 f., 129.
[4] See Appendix II.

India, as seen at sunrise along the banks of the great rivers (see Fig. 29), and in the first prayer, the Gāyatri, which is chanted to "the God behind the Sun" as an orison by every Brahman,[1] despite the later degraded gross poly-

FIG. 29.—"Sun-worship" of the Sumerians at sunrise in modern India.

theism and demonolatry with bloody sacrifices of modern Brahmanism, which have been incorporated from the matriarchist aborigines. And we find colonies of Aryan Sumerian "Fire-worshipping" Magi established on the Indus over two millenniums of years before the traditional date for Zoroaster and his Sun-god Ahura-Mazda or Hormzd—a name which I have shown is also derived from the Sumerian. And we now discover the Sumerian origin and source of the Indian Brahmanist tradition that the Sun-god Vishnu had anciently the incarnation and form of a Fish;[2] and is identical with "Dagon" of the Amorite Phœnicians.

[1] W.P.O.B., 264.

[2] See Appendix II.

This Fish divinity or angel, moreover, the so-called "*goddess* Ninā" of Assyriologists (!), is defined not as God himself, but as "Son of God," and as bearing the names of *Pies'* (or *Piesh*) and *Napitub*, which we have seen discloses the Sumerian origin of both names, representation and functions of the Greek and Roman "*Pos*-eidon" and *Neptune*, as well as the Sanskrit *Napat* for "the son of the waters," also the name "Vishnu" (see Appendix II.); and thus adding several more Aryan god-names of Sumerian origin to those already recorded in my former work.[1] These discoveries thus *open up entirely new vistas in the religion of the Sumerians, disclosing the latter as the source of the names, as well as the forms and functions, of the gods of the Aryans.*

It is also of great historical as well as religious significance to discover that *the Death-Amulets of these Aryan Sumero-Phœnicians or Amorites in the Indus Valley have their prayers generally couched in the identical form of the Death-Amulets of the Early Sumerians*[2] (*hitherto overlooked by Assyriologists*) *and of the "Cup-marked Script" of the Early Sumerian amulets,*[3] *and of the "Cup-marked" inscriptions in Ancient Britain.* And they strikingly confirm my readings of these Cup-marked inscriptions on Sumerian amulets and on the prehistoric monuments of Ancient Britain, which I have proved were erected by the blood-ancestors of the Britons, properly so-called, the Sumero-Phœnicians.

The excavation of the nests of these actual Death-Amulets and signet seals of famous Vedic sages, priestesses and princes from the masonry ruins which included visible graves, implies that these were the actual tombs and formerly sacred shrines of most of the famous personages whose names are inscribed on the seals, and that "Cæsar's dust" has been exhumed. It would thus be only fitting that on completion of the excavations a suitable memorial be erected to mark the sacred spot where rested the earthly remains of such

[1] W.P.O.B., 242, etc. [2] *Ib.*, 255 f., 411 f. [3] *Ib.*, 238 f.

famous Vedic Aryan pioneers of Indian civilization and religion.

The remarkable historicity of the Indian Epic and Vedic records of the Ancient Aryan kings and sages, as authentic and independent sources of new Sumerian history—a fact which I have disclosed and proved in my former work—is also further established by these seals. Not only do the Vedas and the Indian Epic King-lists, as far as they go, supply an *unique* key to the original form of the names of the Sumerian and later Mesopotamian and Hittite kings, but they fill up and illumine, as we have found, many blank and dark places in Sumerian history ; and they supply a key to the symbolism on Sumerian seals and monuments which has hitherto been inexplicable to Assyriologists, as I have freely shown in my former work, and in the present one in regard to Lord Mudgala's seal of Edin, and Sushena's and other seals.

The fictitiousness of the majority of the names of Sumerian and other Early Mesopotamian kings as " restored " by Assyriologists, obsessed with false racial and religious theories, and without any key to the proper form of the personal names written in the polyphonous Sumerian and cuneiform script, is also amply evident. The result of this wholesale conjectural coining of fictitious names has been to grossly mislead students of Comparative History, Philologists, Anthropologists and Archæologists. I speak somewhat feelingly on this subject, as no one has suffered more seriously, and had so many laborious years of research needlessly wasted, than I have had by too confidingly accepting those false names thus dogmatically put forward by accredited " Established Authority."

And the fact is abundantly established by these seals that their authors were of the same Aryan Sumero-Phœnician race which, as I have conclusively proved, civilized, colonized and Aryanized Ancient Albion, and who were blood-ancestors of the Britons. And we have found that the first king of the Aryan Phœnicians, already about 3100 B.C., called himself "Ruler of the Waves."

Finally, it would be futile to pretend ignorance that in these matters, led by the new facts, I am at opposite poles from "leading authorities"; and yet the situation is not altogether without its compensations. One who comes to history without prejudice is more likely than the other sort to be guided in right directions by its facts as to points with respect to which certainty is difficult of attainment, and as to which, when all is said and done, much must in the present state of our knowledge remain obscure. Having no other aim than to advance truth and the general well-being, he is under no temptation to colour facts in the interest either of any particular theory, or of that current sentiment and opinion which it is so necessary that the popular writer should conciliate.

There is after all a real if not very often attained pleasure in helping on the progress of the world without hope of added reward, in promoting by researches into what has been happening in the past the long-drawn effort of our race towards a higher level of health and happiness than that to which the best energies of the "great of old" have been able to raise it. In so doing, we shall show ourselves worthy descendants of those Aryan ancestors to whose genius we are mainly indebted for what "Higher Civilization" we at present enjoy; and shall haply in looking back on our brief passage over the planet escape the misery, to which so many must in these days be exposed, of regretting the trivial and ephemeral character of the occupations in which we have engaged. For in all true Progress, in these too self-complacent times, in industrial and social life, free institutions and ethics, science and art,

"The Message for the Future
Is the Message of the Past."

APPENDICES

I

"URUAS'-THE-KHĀD" (OR PHŒNICIAN) AS PROPER NAME AND TITLE OF THE EARLY SUMERIAN KING "UR-NINĀ" SO-CALLED, THE FOUNDER OF FIRST PANCH(-ĀLA) OR PHŒNICIAN DYNASTY ABOUT 3100 B.C.

THE proofs for the reading of *Uruas'* for the first part of the name of the great Early Sumerian King of Lagash, in Mesopotamia and of Edin of the Indus Valley, hitherto arbitrarily called "Ur-Ninā" by Assyriologists, and his identity with the Early Aryan king of the Indian Epics *Haryas'wa*, the founder of the First Panch(-āla) or Phœnician Dynasty, have been cited in the text. Not only does "Uruas'" literally equate with "Haryas'wa" of the Aryan Epic King-lists, but he occupies the same relative position in those lists, and his descendants bear substantially the same names as those of Uruas' in the Mesopotamian King-lists. Moreover, this identity is absolutely clinched by the secondary title of King Uruas' as *Barama-'hās* being paralleled by the Vedic and Epic title of *B'armyas'wa* for Haryas'wa; and even the *Uru* of the first part of his Sumerian name has radically the same literal meaning in Sumerian as *Hary* has in the Sanskrit.[1]

The second part of the name or title of King Uruas', namely, that read as "Ninā" by Assyriologists, is now found evidently to read "*Khād*" or "*Kūad*," and thus further confirms his identity as a Phœnician.

On revising the spelling of the so-called "Ninā" portion of the name in the original inscriptions of Uruas' and his descendants, I observed that ***the bilingual Akkadian glossaries gave no Sumerian phonetic values*** for this compound word-sign, which Assyriologists have, notwithstanding, rendered "*Ninā*" from one of its Assyrian Semitic synonyms, as the name for Nineveh. I then observed that while the glossaries give no Sumerian phonetic value for this sign they nevertheless call the sign itself "S'a-es'-s'i(-ku) *Ku-u-a-di* kiki."[2] This syllabic spelling reads: "S'aes's'i *Kūadi* kiki," and means literally, "The dwelling[3] of the *Kūadi* of the Sun,"[4] and thus presumably by the affix *Kiki*, or "cities," associates the people of the *Kūadi* cities with the Sun cult.

The word "Kūadi" in this compound word-sign—a sign which first

---

[1] *Uru* in Sumerian="dog" in sense of "hero" (B., 11260; M., 8634), disclosing Sumerian source of the English "hero" and in the Sumerian a lion is "the great *Uru* (or dog)." Now *Hary* in Sanskrit also means "lion" (M.W.D., 1292).

[2] B., 4803.

[3] *Kiki*, or "city" duplicated, is given the synonym of *Uru*, or "dwelling," B., 9808.

[4] *S'aes's'i* is obviously the syllabic spelling of *S'es'i*, the dual Sun, S'amas' (B., 10237–8); the suffix *ku* is placed after loan words when written by Semite Babylonians and does not form a phonetic of the word. Cp. L.S.G., 25.

appears in the documents of King Uruas' and presumably coined by him —now suggested that it designated the "*Kadi* or *Gadi*" title which I had found was a favourite title of the Phœnicians.[1]

The further examination of this compound sign in question now confirmed this Phœnician application. This name "*Kūadi*" as the essential part of this word-sign name, now suggested that that compound sign (the so-called "Ninā"), which consists of a Fish (*Kūa* or *Kha*) within the pictograph sign for a House (with the meaning of "house, ocean and father"), was presumably a compound of the two well-known Sumerian word-signs *Kūa* or *Kha* (Fish) + *ad* (Father-protector of the House), and thus, giving the phonetic form of *Kūād* or *Khād*. And this meaning of "Father of the House of the Fish" or "Father of the Ocean" was a fitting title for the founder of the First Dynasty of the Phœnician mariners, who as I have shown in my former work were the blood ancestors of the Early Britons, whose descendants have been styled, "The Ruler of the Waves"; but which title is now seen to have been used by an Early Sumero-Phœnician ancestor before 3000 B.C.

The "House," or "Father" sign, inside of which is placed the Fish, is usually written in this compound sign in the simple form of the ordinary "House" sign *Ab*, with the meaning also of "Father" and "Ocean"; and differing from the *Ad* "Father" or "House-protecting Father" sign by the absence of the two cross strokes for the weapon of the protecting father. This usual absence of these two extra strokes within this sign is perhaps owing to want of space by the lapidary in cutting more lines than those of the Fish with its fins and tail, or partly owing to the fins occupying most of the space usually occupied by these cross lines; or it may be that as both signs meant "father" in association with "House" the two signs *Ab* and *Ad* were considered interchangeable. But in the famous genealogical limestone plaque of Uruas'[2] at least, the cross strokes of the *Ad* sign seem evident in this sign in question; and so also in some of his son's (Bidasnadi) documents there are more internal strokes than those required for the Fish and its fins and tail, and thus represent the *Ad* sign in the compound *Kūa-ad* or *Kha-ad, i.e.,* "*Khād.*" And this value for this "Ninā" sign is positively established by the Sumerian phonetic value for the name of this sign as "The dwelling of the *Kūadi* of the Sun" above cited.

This *Kūadi* or *Khādi* or *Khad* value for this sign thus discloses the Sumerian original of the *Kadi, Kad* or *Gad* title of the Phœnicians as "the sons of Haryas'wa" (the Khād), as "The able *Panch*" are repeatedly called in later times. It discloses also the Sumerian source of the Phœnician name "*Qad-esh*" or "*Kad-esh*" as "House of the Kads," a favourite title for Phœnician settlements and the source of the name *Gades* for the old Phœnician seaport outside the Mediterranean, the modern Cadiz. It also discloses the source and meaning of the name "Sea of the *Quadi*" the name applied by the Ancient Egyptians to the Sea of the Levant and the Eastern Mediterranean,[3] as the especial haunt of the Phœnician mariners of Kadesh and Syria-Phœnicia and Asia Minor; and "Frith of the Gads" the Roman "Fretum Gadita" for the Straits of Gibraltar.

The name appears in the Indian Epics as *Cedi* or *Chedi*, as a title of descendants of Haryas'wa, the Panch(-āla) or Phœnician.[4] And we have found that the Aryan Phœnicians actually employed *Kad* and *Gad* as a title on their Sumerian seals in the Indus Valley.

For further evidence of this *Khād* value for this word hitherto read "Ninā" see App. II.

---

[1] See previous notes in text. [2] Déc., pl. 2 *bis*, no. 1.

[3] Cp. Budge, *Egyptian Dict.*, 142 and 1045, wherein the final *d* of the Egyptian text is transliterated *t*.

[4] W.P.O.B., 168, 262.

II

The so-called "Goddess Ninā" of Assyriologists is the Sun-Fish or Resurrecting Sun of the Father-god Induru, invoked in the Sumerian seals of the Indus Valley; and Vishnu, the Sea-god Poseidon or Neptune (Napat), "Dagon" of the Philistines, and the Fish-emblem of Christ.

When the word-sign hitherto read "Ninā" (discussed in Appendix I.) occurs in the inscriptions of King Uruas' and his successors with the prefix "lord, divine, or god" (*as'*), as a divinity, it is called by Assyriologists "The goddess Ninā"; and King Uruas' (Ur-Ninā) and his successors are credited with having worshipped this goddess and with having erected many temples to her and images of her.

As the worship of goddesses was a cult of the unregenerate aborigines of Chaldea and elsewhere, and so wholly at variance with what I had observed regarding the exalted monotheistic religion of the Early Aryans or "Sumerians" and of the Early Phœnicians in particular (to whom Uruas' and his dynasty belonged), and who I had found were essentially monotheists and worshippers of the Father-god Ia, or Induru, with his twin angels of the two-phased Sun, I re-examined the evidence for the alleged Sumerian worship of goddesses, as far as my time permitted. But, so far, I have failed to find unequivocal proof that the Early Sumerians worshipped any goddesses at all.[1] The masculine gender and merely angelic character of this so-called "Ninā" we shall see presently. The so-called "Is'i-tar," worshipped by Sargon I. was, I found, not "Ishtar" but a title of the Father-god as "Baptiser" (*S'akhar*), and so with others of the alleged early female divinities of the Sumerians. On the other hand the non-Sumerian Semites and Chaldees were notorious worshippers of the Moon and the Mother-Son Pantheon, demanding bloody sacrifices, which were abhorrent to the Sun cult. And some of the later Sumerians, such as Gudia, the Ur and Erech Dynasties, etc., no doubt incorporated into the pure Sun cult of the Sumerians much of the matriarchist cult of the aboriginal "Semitic" Chaldees.

Prof. Sayce appears to be one of the first who identified this supposed "goddess Ninā" of Uruas' and his Sumerian successors with the goddess Ishtar of the Semites. He says: "*Nina* and *Nana* are dialectic forms of the same word" . . . "the goddess Nāna means 'the divine lady'"[2] . . . "Nāna does not appear to have been replaced by the name *Istar* until after the beginning of the Semitic period."[3] Prof. Langdon fully accepts this Ninā of the Sumerians as a goddess, and as the Sumerian form of Ishtar, her name meaning, he says, "Queen of the waters";[4] and he makes her "the sister of Ningirsu, 'Lord of the freshets,' a type of Tammuz worshipped at Lagash"; and he devotes many pages to the identification of Ninā with Nanā, a Chaldean form of Ishtar.

Now let us see what the Sumerian texts say about this so-called "goddess Ninā." One of the earliest mentions of the name of the divinity thus read

---

[1] Goddesses seem absent in Early Sumerian seals and monuments. Statues of the wives of some of the early and of contemporary kings are referred to; and some of these kings were given the divine prefix, but presumably in sense of "Lord" only. It seems a question whether the Nin-khar-sag of "Enannatum" is not his own mother, afterwards deified by the Chaldees. It is possible he may have patronized goddesses of his subject Chaldees.

[2] *Hibbert Lects.*, 116–7.

[3] *Ib.*, 260.

[4] *Tammuz and Ishtar*, 1914, 45.

"Ninā" is in the same document of King Uruas', in which he records his building of "the two Edins." This record on a stone tablet[1] states, according to Radau's translation made on the supposition that Ninā was a goddess:[2] "Ur-Ninā, king of Shirpurla, the son of Gunidu, son of Gursar, the house of *Ninā* has built. The (image of) *Ninā* he has renewed, two statues [canal][3] he has digged Ninā's statue [canal] for the declaring of her (his ?) name[4] the Apir he has renewed. Forty servants of his wife for *Ninā*[5] that called him to be her prince [*Bar* seer], two Edins he caused to build."

There is nothing in all this which necessarily implies that "Ninā" was a goddess, rather than a "god." The forty "servants of his wife" chosen by him for service on Ninā—which sentence is translated by M. Thureau-Dangin as "he chose by lot forty . . . spouses of Ninā," were doubtless "the slave-girl" priestesses or vestals of the Sun-temple of which we have seen Us'ij was the chief at Edin. And indeed the terming of women as "spouses" to a divinity, implies that the latter was masculine. The words translated variously, "servants of his wife (sic !)" or "spouses" are *ur dam*, wherein *dam* or "spouse" is disclosed as Sumerian origin of English "*dam*" and "dame." And it is significant that Uruas' here calls himself "the *Bar* seer"[6] of this divinity, *i.e.*, *Baru* or Brahman Seer; just as we have seen he called himself "Brahman" and "Seer" in his Edin seal already cited and translated.

The notion that "Ninā" was the name of a Sumerian "goddess," while assumed from its general similarity to the name of the aboriginal Chaldean Mother-goddess, was supposed to be confirmed by a divine name read "*Nin-a-a*" on Akkad and later inscriptions. Thus Sargon's son Manishtusu dedicates a mace-head to a divinity read as "Nin-a-a," wherein *Nin*, however, is written *not* by the Fish-house-Father sign, but by the compound sign of "Woman and weapon"—the latter having no less than about twenty different polyphonous values !

The occurrence, however, of the "woman" sign in phonetic spelling of compound personal names, does not imply that these persons were necessarily females. On the contrary, it occurs in spelling various titles of Ia or Induru (Indra), the Sun-god and most of the male gods of the Chaldean pantheon. Indeed, the second part of the name "Nin-a-a" is unequivocally male and not female. For *A-a*, meaning "Of the Waters," is the actual title of the "Fish-man-god" as figured on an ancient Hitto-Sumerian seal (see W.O.P.B., 247, fig. 36), and is nowhere clearly applied to a goddess by Sumerians so far as I have found. It is the *A* name for Vishnu in Sanskrit.

Moreover, as the Akkads and later Sumerians were in the habit of spelling phonetically the same personal name by different syllabic signs, and the vowels freely interchanged, this "Nin" word-sign was probably used, I think, for *Nun*, a common Sumerian name for Ia or Induru as "The Fish-man god," and apparently derived from the Chaldean *Nunnu* "a fish." And as the final consonant in Sumerian syllables frequently drops out, this *Nun* may become "Nin"; and in the Isin king-list in App. IV. "Ur-Nina" is actually called "Ur *Nun*." And this "Nun," as I have shown, is obviously the Sumerian original of the Ancient Egyptian name *Nu* for the "god of the Waters"—who indeed is called *Nu* in Sumerian[7]

---

[1] Déc., pl. 2, no. 2. Transl. R., 62 f.; T.D.I., 13.

[2] R.B., 61 f. [3] "Canal," T.D.I., 13.

[4] T.D.I. reads this sentence, "and to Ninā dedicated (this canal)."

[5] T.D.I. reads this, "he chose by lot the forty . . . spouses of Ninā."

[6] *Bar-bi-pad*, wherein the *Bar* is written by the Bar word-sign of the Indus seals which formed the first part of the name Bar-ama; but *Bar* itself = "priest"; and *pad* = see, recognize, speak" (B., 9412) and its prefix *bi* also = "speak, perceive," B., 5124; M., 3473, etc., and thus the word means "Seer."

[7] Howardy, *op. cit.*, 69, p. 43.

—and of the Greek *Nōe*, the Hebrew *Noh*, whence our "Noah" for the legendary boatman of the Flood-waters of the Deep; as well as secondarily of the Eddic Gothic *Nōa* or *Noi* "a ship," Indo-Persian *Nau* "a ship" and our "Navy." Thus the god-name read *Nin-a-a* (which also reads *Ni-a-a* or *I-a-a*)[1] would read: "The god Nun (Nin, Ni, or Ia) of the Waters," and thus identify him with *Kha-ad*, "The Father-fish," and *Su'-kha*, the Sun-Fish of our seals.

Indeed, the very same compound sign of "Woman and weapon" with the ideogram *Nin* is also given the values of *Ia* (*i.e.*, Indara) and *Ni*; and with the divine prefix it is defined in the glossaries as "Ia (or Ni), the *Net* of the Waters" (*Ia* (or *Ni*) *sa-a*)[2]; and we shall see in Appendix III. that "The Net of the Waters" was a title of the Sun-Fish Khād. And it is further defined there as "The *Male* of the Flood Waters" (*Ni-tax ra*).[3] This unequivocally disposes of the "goddess" theory of "Ninā" by the reading of its "woman" sign for its spelling and meaning.

Now as regards the positive evidence against the Sumerian reading of "Ninā" for the "Fish-house-Father" sign, which we have found reads "Kuad or Khād," in App. I. Further, direct evidence for the reading "Khād," besides that cited there, is found in the glossaries which define the "Fish-god" as "The god *Kha-ad* called *Su* or *Zu*,"[4] wherein the word "god" seems rendered by *Gud*, thus disclosing probably the origin of the Gothic *gud* (or *guth*), the source of our English word "God." This Fish-god is moreover defined as "The god Water-cutter, companion of the sceptre-(holding) Induru."[5] Thus the Fish-god *Kha* called *Su* gives the equivalence of *Su-Kha* with *Kha-ad* or *Khād*, as the name of that god, and the "S'u-kha" of the seals.

Further, the Fish-god is defined as "The Fish-god of Bel (Father-god) the enterer (of the Waters of Rebirth ?),"[6] and this is explained as "The god *Na-pi-tub*,"[7] which thus discloses the Sumerian origin of the Roman sea-god's name of "Neptune," as well as the Vedic Sanskrit *Napat* or "son of the Waters"—the Greek "Poseidon" coming from the other synonym of Pies' as we have seen.

The definition of this Fish-House sign *Kuād* in the glossaries as "The *cities* (kiki) of the House of the Fish of the Sun" presumably relates to the numerous Phœnician cities called "Kad-esh" or "House of the Kad," evidently deriving their name from the sacred Fish of the Sun-temple therein as "The House of the Kūadi of the Sun." This also would explain why in late Syrio-Phœnician the word "Kadesh" means "holy."

The Phœnician Sun-temple at the old Phœnician port of Abdera in Spain (the Abdara of Ptolemy, which I have shown was "the *Kaptara*-Land" beyond the Upper Sea or Mediterranean of the lately found edict of Sargon I.),[8] displays on its representation on Phœnician coins *two of the four pillars of its façade in the shape of a Fish*.[9] And this sacred Sun-Fish of the Phœnicians now explains the Fish on the coins of Gades with its famous Sun-temple associated with Hercules of the Phœnicians.

This Sumerian name for "Fish" (*Kha*), with its sacred solar associations, although it has dropped out of use in Sanskrit as a term for "Fish," never-

---

[1] On value *Ia*, see B., 5325, etc. *Yahva* title of Indra=Hebrew Yahvh.

[2] B., 10982. On *sa* "net" B., 3083.

[3] B., *ib.*, *Vax-tax*, B., 6106; "male" B., 5022.

[4] U (or Gud) *kha-ad* me su (or *zu*) B., 11839. On *U* or *Gud*="god," M., 4301.

[5] U kud tab khat nu, B., *ib.* On *kud*="cutter of water," M., 271; and *Nu* as Induru, see before; and Howardy, *Clavis Cuneorum*, No. 69, p. 43.

[6] As' kha sig su, B., 11837. On *Sig*=god Bel, B., 3378; and *su*="enter," B., 166.

[7] As' na-pi-tub, B., 11837, wherein *tub* sign has meaning of "son," M., 2605.

[8] W.P.O.B., 413–14.

[9] J. Y. Akerman, *Ancient Coins*, pl. 2.

theless appears to survive in religious terms in Sanskrit, as *Kha* for "The Sun," "Heaven" and "Supreme Spirit"; [1] and as the unaspirated *Ka*, meaning "The Sun" and "Sun-god Vishnu." [2] And it also accounts for the Indian Brahmanist tradition that long ago the Sun-god assumed the form of a Fish in the Fish incarnation of Vishnu, in which he subdued the Serpent of the Deep.

The effigy of this Sun-Fish, as a Fish-man, or as a Fish, is figured on the Sumerian, Hitto-Phœnician and Babylonian sacred seals,[3] as well as on the prehistoric monuments of the Ancient Britons.[4] In addition to the examples of the latter, instanced in my former work, there is a good sculpture of the worship of this Sun-Fish in the Cross of Kells, in County Meath (M. Keane, *Towers and Temples of Anc. Ireland*, 1867, Fig. 25). And it was presumably this ancient "pagan" Sun-Fish, the *Piesh* or Vishnu, which formed the legendary leviathan of the Deep called "*Peishta Mor*" or "The great *Peishta*," [5] which St Patrick slew in Ireland.

And this Resurrecting Sun-Fish of the Sumerians and the "Dagon" of the Philistines was presumably the Aryan source of the symbol of a Fish for Christ, among the early Christians, a large proportion of whom were Syria-Phœnicians of Galilee of the Gentiles. And the destruction of its effigy by St Patrick was merely in series with the wholesale destruction of beautiful pre-Christian crosses by the early Church throughout the British Isles, merely because they were "pagan," or pre-Christian. And the *Piscina* or "Fish-bowl" built on the south side of the altar in old Christian churches in Britain and elsewhere is evidently a survival of the Sumero-Phœnician Fish shrine of this pagan "Sun-Fish of the Resurrection and the Life" invoked in these seals.

This Sun-Fish was also called "The Net of God" by the Sumerians and Indo-Aryans as noted in Appendix III.

III

The Sun-Fish as "The Net of God" of Sumerians and Indo-Aryans and in (?) Christianity.

The Sun-Fish of these seals is also called by Sumerians "The Fish Lord of Bel," [6] *The Net* of entry [to the Waters of Rebirth ?]; [7] and under this title he is given the same explanatory title of "*Na-pi-tub*" (or "Neptune") as before.[8] The word for "net" here is the same word which is used by the great Sumero-Phœnician conqueror Bi(d)as'nadi (the Pasenadi or Prasenajit of the Indian records and the "Eannatum" of Assyriologists), the son of Mudgala and grandson of Uruas'-the-Khad, in his celebrated monument of victory generally called the "Stele of the Vultures," on account of the vultures figured on it or carrying off the limbs of the dead foes. In this, in reciting his treaty with the chief of his vanquished enemies, "the men of Umma or Gishkhu he calls himself 'The great Net of the Setting Sun and Rising Sun'" [9] and repeats the phrase several times and invokes

---

[1] M.W.D., 334. [2] *Ib.*, 240.

[3] W.P.O.B., 247, 251. [4] *Ib.*, 308.

[5] S. Baring-Gould, *Lives of the Saints*, Mar. 306.

[6] The Father-god Induru or Indra.

[7] As' kha sig sa tur. B., 11838. On *sa*=net, B., 3085; *tur*=enter, B., 1072.

[8] B., 11838.

[9] Sa sus'-gal as' ra (or *utu*). *Sa* is translated by Radau as "scourge" (R.B., 76), but see note 2.

the vengeance of the Net on those who may break the treaty. And he figures on that monument (see Fig. 32, p. 41), which is a picture gallery in itself, a group of his prisoners caught in this wide-meshed Net. And incidentally it is to be noted that in consummating this treaty with the people of Umma city-state he sacrificed "two doves" and "young oxen"—this however may have been to pander to the superstitions of the other party to the treaty, as Alexander was in the habit of doing.

This title of "The Net" for this Fish of the Resurrecting Sun now appears to disclose the Sumerian source and explanation of the worship of the Net by Babylonians referred to in the Old Testament, which states: "They (the Chaldeans) sacrifice unto their net, and burn incense unto their drag;"[1] though it is evident from the comment of the Hebrew writer thereon that he did not understand this alien symbolism. And it also seems to be referred to by Christ: "The kingdom of heaven is like unto a net."[2]

Amongst Indo-Aryans, we find "Holder of the Net"[3] as the name of one of "The Sons of the Sky or Dawn" (Aditya) in Brahmanism. And in Indian Buddhism, one of "the beautiful names" of Buddha is "The Net,"[4] and I possess an image of Buddha inscribed with this name for him in Tibetan and Sanskrit of the Chenlung period.

IV

First Phœnician Dynasty of Uruas' ("Ur-Ninā") discovered as "First Erech Dynasty" of Isin King-lists; and "Gilgamesh" or Gis'zax (Caxus) of Erech as father of Uruas' (Haryas'wa) and historical original of Hercules of the Phœnicians about 3150 B.C.

The new King-lists of the Isin period about 2050 B.C., recorded on a cuneiform clay "prism" in the Weld-Blundell Collection at Oxford,[5] purport to give a complete list of the kings and dynasties of Mesopotamia with their regnal years extending back to 241,000 years "before the Flood" (!). Professor Langdon on failing to find in this semi-fabulous list the names either of "Ur Nina" or any of his dynasty, or those of most of the famous Sumerian kings, including the great Gudea (Gadhi), who were the authors of by far the greater part of the innumerable monuments and records which make up Sumerian history, instead of remarking as one would expect on the apparent shortcomings of this list compiled by the credulous later priests of the insignificant Isin dynasty—a petty dynasty of reputedly alien origin, which appears after the devastating raid by Elam which destroyed the Ur Dynasty, and which has left no monuments but only a few inscribed bricks, two nails, and these king-lists—on the contrary he confidently accepts this Isin list as more authoritative than the actual contemporary records of the great kings themselves, and rejecting the latter declares that these kings were impostors in calling themselves "kings" and dynasties, merely because he could not find them in his Isin list.[6]

On scanning this Isin list, however, it appeared to me that not only were "Ur Nina" and his dynasty recorded therein, but that they were given the very first place in the list of human dynasties, where the supernatural ages end and the natural human ages begin. This observation was based on the general similarity in the form of several of the names, their relative order

---

[1] Hab., i, 16.
[2] Mat., xiii, 47.
[3] Jālan-dhara.
[4] Jāla.
[5] Weld-Blundell Collect. Cuneiform Texts, 1923, II, 2 f., by S. Langdon.
[6] *Ib.*, 7 f.

FIRST PHŒNICIAN DYNASTY OF URUAS' ("UR-NINA") AS "FIRST ERECH DYNASTY" OF ISIN KING-LISTS.

1st Erech Dynasty of Isin lists.		1st Phœnician Dynasty of Uruas'.		Indian Epic Lists Lunar (Yadu). Solar (S.).
As revised by me.	*As read by Prof. Langdon.*	*As revised by me.*	*Read by Assyriologists.*	
1. URU-AS' nun-gal.	Ur Nun-gal.	URU-AS' Kha-ad.	Ur-Ninā.	HARYAS'WA.
2. Ab-bi unu-ma.	Utul-kalam-ma.	A Mad-gal.	Akurgal.	Mudgala.
3. La BI-S'E[-na-di]er.	La-ba-s'e-ir.	BI(D)-AS'-na-di.	Eannatum.	PASENADI or Badhryas'-wa.
4. In-nun-nad AS'-NA (br. of 3 ?)	En-nun-nad-an-na.	In AS'NA-di.	Enannatum.	YUWAN-AS'WA (S.).
5. TA-AR-IS-U (s. of 3?).	. . . ge-de.	Ene TAR-SI.	Enetarzi.	Divo DĀSA, TRASA-DASYU (S.).
6. ME-DE as'-na.	Me-lam-an-na.	(Lugal As'-da kad, in Lagash.)	Lugal Anda.	Mitrāyu or METTIYO.
7. Lugal KI-AGA.	Lugal Ki-aga.	Uru KA-GI-na.	Urukagina.	King CYA-vana.
End of Dynasty.	*End of Dynasty.*	*End of Dynasty.*	*End of Dynasty.*	*End of Dynasty.*

and number, and the point at which both dynasties end by war. And further examination completely confirmed this identity for all the names.

In the annexed table I give the kings' names of this dynasty in question, which is represented as the " First Dynasty of Urug or Erech," alongside the names of the dynasty of Uruas' from their own monuments, for comparison. In column 1 are given the kings' names in the Isin list as revised by me, in column 2 the names as read by Professor Langdon, while in columns 3 and 4 are the names of the First Phœnician Dynasty, in my revision and that of Assyriologists respectively, and in column 5 the names from the Indian Epics and Vedas. It will be seen from columns 2 and 4 that the first-named king on the Isin list, Ur Nun-gal, suggests " Ur Nina " of the Phœnician list—*Nin* being as we have seen a Semitic dialectic variant of *Nun*; that the 4th Ennunnadanna suggests " Enannatum " the 4th in the Phœnician list, and the 7th and last Kiaga suggests " Prince *Kagina*," the 7th and last on the Phœnician list.

On revising the spelling of the names on this Isin list, I found that the 1st reads " Uru-as' Nun-gal " or " Uruas' the great Fish," and thus obviously is a slightly variant synonym of Uruas'-the-Khād (or Fish-house-Father), the founder of the First Phœnician dynasty. The 2nd reads " Ab-bi unu-ma " or " The Protector of Oxen (or Herdsman), the priest of the Land," [1] and thus is clearly a title for Mudgala of the vast herds of kine on the Indus, and he is actually called " Lord of Cattle " in his Vedic hymn, he was also a high-priest and Vedic singer, and the 2nd of the Phœnician dynasty. The 3rd reads " La *Bi-s'e* er " or " The Protector *Bi-s'e*, the hurrier or capturer," which is evidently a shortened title of Bi(d)as'nadi as the great conqueror, and the 3rd of that dynasty. The 4th, " In-nun-nad As'-na " was apparently In As'nadi the brother of the 3rd of the Lagash lists. The 5th, which is defaced, seems to read " Ta-ar-is-u," [2] and so is a Semitic form of Tarsi, the 5th emperor of the Phœnician dynasty, omitting the two local rulers of Lagash (Entemena and In As'nadi II.). The 6th, Me-de-As'-na, is evidently the son and successor of the "divine Tarsi" (Divo-Dāsa), named *Mitrayu* (Pali *Mettiyo*) in the Indian lists. The 7th " Lugal Kiaga " or " King Kiaga," is evidently " Prince [3] Kagina " of the Lagash lists, and " King Cya-vana " of the Vedas and Indian Epics, the son of Mitrayu, and with whom the dynasty ended, just as it ends in the Isin list; and it is significant that this Cyavana is specially called "king" in the Indian lists,[4] just as Kiaga is in this Isin list.[4]

This full and complete agreement between these lists, in the names and titles and relative order clearly establishes the identity of the First Dynasty of Erech of the Isin list with the First Dynasty of the Phœnicians. And it shows that the Sumerians were in the habit, like the Ancient Egyptians, of calling their kings by different names and titles, as I had already observed from the comparison of the different versions, solar and lunar, of the Indian Epic lists.

The coping stone to these proofs is now found in the discovery that the great epic hero and Hercules of the Chaldeans, " *Gilgamesh " of the Semites or Gis'zax* [5] *of the Sumerians*—as my Indian lists show that the name was pronounced by the Sumerians—*was the father of Uruas'* (" *Ur Nina* "), thus gaining for us for the first time the hitherto unknown historical character and date of " Gilgamesh," see his conventional portrait on seal of Sargon I., Fig. 33, p. 47, and in the many other Figs. A, B, C, 30, 33, etc.

The name of the father of Uruas' in this Isin list is read by Professor Langdon as " Gilgamesh." But on revising the spelling I find it reads " As' Gis'-zax

---

[1] *Abhira*=" herdsman " in Sanskrit, and thus presumably derives from this Sumerian *Abbi*.

[2] *Ta-ar*, cp. detailed spelling with B., 359; *u* B., 7773.

[3] *Uru*=" high city prince," Howardy, *op. cit.*, 41, p. 139.

[4] W.V.P., 4, 147.

[5] Or *Izzax*.

ga-mes' "[1] or "Lord Gis'zax the Buffalo (Fire) priest." There is no "*Gil*" or "*Gibil*" in the Sumerian spelling of this name though read so by that scholar; but the Sumerian *Gis'* is given in the glossaries the Semitic equivalent of "Gilgamesh."[2] The use of *ga* for "buffalo" I have already established; and this title of "Buffalo-priest" now explains his usual association with buffaloes, such as his watering these animals (Fig. 33), and his wrestling with wild buffaloes as well as lions, as the Sumerian Hercules, and his wearing the buffalo head, skin, tail and hoof, as so freely figured on seals from the period of Uruas' downwards to the Assyrian period. *Now in the Indian Epics the father of Haryas'wa is called "Caxus" (or Chakshus)* with the epithet of "*Arka*."[3] This "*Caxus*" is now seen to be evidently the Indian form of spelling the Sumerian "Gis'zax" when the writing was converted by the Aryans into alphabetic characters; and "*Arka*" is evidently dialectic for Urug or Erech, the modern *Warka*, the home of "Gilgamesh," and in series with 'Erakles.[4]

Thus "Gilgamesh" the Sumerian "Hercules," and father of the founder of the First Phœnician Dynasty, is now disclosed to be the historical human original of "'Erakles" or "Hercules" of the Phœnicians, with fixed date as an Aryan Sumerian King of about 3150 B.C. Indeed his title *'Erak-les* is now seen to be presumably coined from the name of his ancient capital city *Erech*, Uruk or *Erek*—for the affix *les*, see later.

Uruas' himself writes his father's name repeatedly on his monuments, as do also his descendants, as "*Guni*-tum, son of Gur-sar." Here "Guni-tum" means "Dweller in the place of Fire" (or The Fire-wood brazier)—that is a solar title of high-priest. And significantly his name Gis'zax has the Sumerian synonym of "Gūnni" or "Wood-Fire brazier,"[5] which is spelt with the identical signs used by Uruas' in spelling his father's name, with the addition of the sign for long *u* and duplicated *n*.[6]

Moreover, Gis'zax is given in the Isin list a title,[7] which Professor Langdon translates as "whose father was a fool." Such a title, indeed, would be strange in a dynastic list, especially in regard to one of their greatest heroes, if it really existed. But the "fool" is merely that scholar's own introduction. The text reads clearly *Ab-ba-ni zax la*, and means "whose father was really *Zax*"—Zax or *Sax* or *Sakh* being the common title for the Father-god Indra in the Vedas and Indian literature, where it is spelt *Sakko* in Pali, and *S'akra* in Sanskrit, whilst its *Zax* form, as I have shown in my former work, is evidently the Sumerian origin of the name "Zeus" of the Greeks. My reading is made absolutely certain by the continuation of that sentence in the Isin list,[8] which is read by that scholar as "The lord of Kullab," but which reads unequivocally "Of the seed of the Lord, Father Zax [himself]."[9]

Still further proof of the identity of this portion of the Isin list with the First Phœnician Dynasty and their ancestors is found in the identity in the name of the father (or predecessor) of Gis'zax (or "Gilgamesh") in both the Isin and Indian lists. In the Isin list his name and title is translated by the professor as "The deified Dumuzi, a fisherman."[10] I read it "As' Damuzi s'u-*pur*," or "Lord Damuzi of the hand-bowl (*Pur*)."[11] This

---

[1] *Zax*=Fire-brazier, B., 4577.
[2] M., 4005; B.W., 258.
[3] W.V.P., 4, 144.
[4] Caxus in the mythic portion of the Indian Epics was the father of Caxusha the Manu or patriarch progenitor of the 6th period: and the latter is invoked with "the virtuous one" in a curse in the Atharva Veda, 16, 7, 7.
[5] B., 9690, and cp. P.S.L., 163.
[6] Also spelt syllabically as "Ki-iz-zax," thus equating with "Caxus."
[7] Col. III, l. 18.
[8] *Ib.*, l. 19.
[9] *Kul* "seed," "grandson" B., 1668; M., 943. This discloses Sumer origin of Sanskrit and Hindi, *Kul*, "family," in the sense of descent.
[10] Langdon, *op. cit.*, l. 14, p. 12.
[11] *Pur* "bowl" B., 6971; "totality (abundance)," M., 4952.

apparently correlates the famous magic divining bowl or cauldron of the original Damuzi or Tamuz,[1] with the divining bowl of his later namesake, this "Tamuz," the grandfather of Uruas'. Now in the Indian lists the father of Caxus (*i.e.*, "Gilgamesh") is named *Puru*-jānu,[2] or "The receptacle of production (or creation)," wherein *Puru* or "receptacle" appears to represent the Sumerian *Pur* "bowl"[3] in the Isin title. But another version of the Indian lists actually gives "*Tamas* of the Deep" (Dirgha-*Tamas*, the seer already described in the text), as the grandfather of Haryas'wa (Uruas'),[4] thus giving him the literal equivalent name of the Sumerian "Damuzi" or Tamuz.

It is thus probable that the identity of the Isin and Indian lists may proceed still further back when examined, and that in the former the names up to "The Flood" may prove to be those (or titles) of traditional Aryan or Sumerian kings, to whom fabulous ages have been assigned. But, be this as it may, the fact remains that our new evidence has proved up to the hilt the identity of the human portion of the First Dynasty of Erech of the Isin lists with the First Dynasty of the Phœnicians founded by Uruas', and its Aryan racial character.

The location of King Uruas' (or "Ur Nina") and his dynasty at Uruk or Erech by the Isin lists, and *not* at "Lagash," although against the narrow current theories of Assyriologists, is quite in keeping with the new facts we have elicited regarding the *imperial* character of the dynasty of Uruas'. Thus the grandson of Uruas' is known from the excavated monuments as "King of Kish," the chief capital of Upper Mesopotamia, and as "Emperor of the totality of the Lands," specifying Opis, Elam, S'akh (Indus Valley), etc., etc.; and his son Tarsi was still "King of Kish" and patesi or high-priest of Lagash and victor over Elam. Uruas' himself is, as yet, merely known through the local excavations at his seaport as "King of Lagash" with influence over Eridu, another port to the west; but we have found that he was also "King of Edin" in the Indus Valley. Now, however, in view of his being the son and successor of King Gis'zax (or "Gilgamesh") of Uruk, the "*Caxus* or *Arka*" of the Indian lists, he was doubtless also king of Uruk, the earliest seaport of Mesopotamia, at the modern Warka about 30 miles west of Lagash, and presumably silted up at his epoch, necessitating a new open port such as Lagash. The vast mounds of ruins at Uruk or "Erech," the vastest in all Mesopotamia, *are not yet excavated*, and their excavation has not yet even been begun, except some superficial "scratching" on a spot by Mr Loftus. When the ruins of this ancient city of Uruk or Erech, now disclosed to have been the capital of Hercules of the Phœnicians, are explored in all probability there will be found records of Uruas' (Haryas'wa) designating him "King of Uruk."

This new evidence thus conclusively establishes the fact that the greatest of the Early Sumerian Dynasties, that of Uruas' or "Ur Ninā"—*pace* Professors Langdon and Sayce—was racially Aryan and "Phœnician"; that the father of King Uruas' was the actual historical human original of Hercules-the-Phœnician, the "Gilgamesh" or "Fire-priest" of the Semitic Chaldeans, with relatively fixed date of 3150-3100 B.C., with his capital at Erech; and that this discovery that the Phœnicians were the leading seafaring branch of the Early Sumerians or Aryans, fully confirms the mass of evidence from entirely different sources detailed in my former

---

[1] This bowl seems referred to as S'u-me (or S'u-bur ?) in the Chaldean legend of Tamuz, *e.g.*, Scheil, *Tamuz*, text obv., 2, 15 f.

[2] W.V.P., 4, 144.

[3] Sansk. *Pur* "a receptacle, abundance," M.W.D., 635, thus disclosing the Sumerian origin of *Pur* and *Puru*.

[4] W.V.P., 4, 32-3. Haryas'wa here bears the title of "The Bowman of the Boat" (Dhanwantari) and his son Mudgala the title of "Torch-bearer" (Ketumat)—and we see him carrying the fire-bowl in Fig. 31 (p. 26) upper compartment.

work, proving that the Phœnicians were the Aryan blood-ancestors and the authors of the civilization not only of the Indo-Aryans, but of the Britons and other Phœnician nations in Europe.

V

Izzax (Gis'zax, Sanskrit "Caxus") or "Gilgamesh," heroic King of Erek about 3150 B.C. as human original of "Hercules."

This heroic Aryan king of Erek, the father of King Uruas' or Haryas'wa (the founder of the First Phœnician Dynasty) is credited in the early Sumerian Seals and in later Babylonian legend with performing deeds so generally similar to those of Hercules of the Greeks as to suggest to me that he was the historical human Sumerian source of that legendary hero. And further examination now confirms that identity.

In the annexed table I have compared the leading features of the heroes of these two legends, incorporating the developed legend of the Sumerian hero as current in the later Babylonian epic of about 2000 B.C.

Identity of 'Erakles with Izzax, Gis'zax or "Gilgamesh," King of Erek.

'Erakles	Izzax or Gis'zax of Erek.
Is a solar hero and his Phœnician shrines had Perpetual Fire.	Is a Sun-worshipper and Fire-priest.
Son of Father-god Zeus, to wife of Aryan king.	"Son of Father-god Zax" (Zeus), to wife of Aryan king.
Spurns temptation by goddess of Pleasure.	Spurns temptations by Mother-goddess Ishtar.
Of gigantic stature and strength.	Same.
Twelve chief Labours.	Twelve tablets of his epic associating his deeds with the twelve solar months of year.
Slays devastating Lion by his powerful arms in Nemean grove.	Slays Lion, devastating cattle, by his powerful arms in a grove. (Fig. A, p. xvi.)
Captures sacred Stag.	Overpowers a stag or Antelope. (On seals.)
Captures mad Bull.	Overpowers wild Bull Buffalo. (Figs. B, p. xx.; 30, p. 22; and 36, p. 135.)
Slays a Dragon.	Slays a Dragon (Fig. 35).
Cleanses Augean stables of 3000 oxen by turning on *two* rivers.	Waters oxen by *two* streams of water (Fig. C, p. xxiv.).
Journeyed to far West for golden apples near Pillars of Hercules and gains them.	Journeyed to far West to "The Mountain of Sunset" for plant of Immortality and gains it.
Had as friend the Cen*taur* Phalos who was killed accidentally.	Had as friend the man-Bull (*Taurus*) Enkidu or Eabani who dies prematurely (Fig. 37).
He descended to the world of the Dead and returned alive.	He crossed "The Waters of Death" and returned alive.
Clad in Lion's skin with head.	Has leonine head in seals.
Carries sometimes a club.	Carries sometimes a spiked beam (Fig. 38).
Was not worshipped as a god.	Was not worshipped as a god.
Honoured especially by Phœnicians, and as ancestor.	His cult begun by 1st Dynasty of Phœnicians, and as ancestor.

It thus appears that the later Greek poets and mythmongers took the old Sumerian tradition of this heroic King of Erek and embroidered it into the graceful legend such as we now know it. And they gave him the epithet of " '*Erakles* " or " Hercules " presumably from the name of his capital Erek or Urug—just as he is called in the Indian Epics " *Arka* " (of " Erek or *Warka* ")—and they seem to have added the epic Greek affix of *lis* or *lies* " a lion, " to designate him as " The Lion of Erek."

FIG. 35.—Izzax (Hercules) killing the Dragon. From seal-impression of Dukgin (" Dungi "), about 2350 B.C. (After Ward, 51.)

Note the *sa* or *gal* word-sign in third column from right has its stem of the crown at one end as in Seal VI., p. 65.

This epic Greek affix *Lis* " a lion " is now disclosed to be derived from the Sumerian *Lig* or *Lik* " a great dog (*i.e.* lion) or hero " (B. 11251 f.), which survives in the Greek *Lykos* " a wolf," *i.e.* the wild dog and parent of the dog. Our English word " Wolf," moreover, derived immediately from the Gothic *ulf* or *wulf*, is now seen to be cognate with " whelp " and derived from the Sumerian Chaldee synonym for this same word-sign *Kalbu* (B. 11248), from which the initial *K* has dropped out, as in " Hatti " for " Khatti," etc.—*b* and *f* being freely interchangeable. Whilst " Kelpie " for the wolf-headed sprite of the streams retains the fuller *Kalbu* form. Thus again we find the radically Aryan character of the Sumerian language.

FIG. 36.—Izzax slaying the Lion and overpowering the mad Bull. From a seal of about 2700 B.C. of Uruas'-ban, high-priest of " The city of the Sun-Fish " (Adab).

(After seal in Chicago Field Museum, in Bank's *Bismya*, 303.)

FIG. 37.—The "Centaur" Eabani or Enkidu, friend of Izzax of Erek, carrying the "Celtic" Sun-Cross standard, as the Centaur Phalos, friend of 'Erakles. From Seal in N.Y. Metrop. Museum. (After Ward, 454.)

FIG. 38.—Izzax of Erek with "Club" as Sumerian source of 'Erakles with his club. From Seal of about 2500 B.C. (After Heuzey and Ward, 286.)

INDEX

ABBREVIATIONS: A.B. = Ancient Britain; I.V. = Indus Valley; k. = king; n. = name; p. = priest; S. = Sumerian; Skt. = Sanskrit.

PRINTED IN GREAT BRITAIN BY
THE EDINBURGH PRESS, 9 AND 11 YOUNG STREET, EDINBURGH

The long-lost origins of our ancestors, the Briton, Scots and Anglo-Saxons in the prehistoric and pre-Roman periods back to about 3000 B.C., are now recovered to a great extent in the present work by means of newly discovered historical evidence. Those ancestors are now found to be, not savages, but a highly civilized and literate race, pioneers of civilization and a branch of the famous Phœnicians, who were not Semites, as hitherto supposed, but fair long-headed Aryans in race, speech and script, and identical with the Sumerians. These discoveries are founded on a mass of inscriptions, including hitherto undeciphered Phœnician and Sumerian inscriptions in Britain, and uninterpreted inscriptions and emblems on Early Briton coins of the pre-Roman period. Our ancestral British patron saints, folk-lore and national emblems are found to be Phœnician, and about fifty per cent. of our common English words are disclosed to be Sumerian (Cymrian or Cumbrian), and the Sumerians proved to be the long lost Early Aryans.—*From the Preface.*

Dramatic confirmation of these discoveries has just come in the large "finds" of Sumerian seals of about 3000 B.C. unearthed in the Indus Valley, a few weeks ago, disclosing the Sumerians as the Early Aryans—a discovery first announced and established in this book.

CONTENTS

CONTENTS (*continued*)

APPENDICES

SOME EARLY PRESS OPINIONS.

A most interesting book. It certainly appears to scratch out the "pre" from the so-called "prehistoric" period in which the origin of our island-ancestors was deemed "lost."—*Daily Mail.*

Offers good reading—subject treated with insight and given attractive form. —*Oxford Chronicle.*

Never before has the Phœnician theory of the Britons been presented so authoritatively and supported by such an imposing array of evidence.—*Northern Whig.*

One is almost constrained to believe the new theory. It provokes thought, and it ought to stimulate research into regions not sufficiently explored. We may be sure that many theories formulated and accepted in the past, even by careful and learned historians, will have to be abandoned.—*Inquirer.*

Is nothing short of a real romance—a book you have to tear yourself away from. Profusely and well illustrated—a fascinating book.—*Birmingham Gazette.*

A book of remarkable and unusual interest, written in a very interesting manner. The facts and explanations are very striking and fill over 400 pages, interspersed with drawings of the monuments, coins, stone relics, ancient inscriptions, &c.—*Newcastle Chronicle.*

Fascinating deductions of stimulating interest. The claim is all the more interesting because it approaches the subject from a new angle.—*Western Morning News.*

Proofs as convincing as they are laboriously worked out.—*Daily Graphic.*

The glory of descent from pure British stock has been greatly enhanced by an archæological feat of the first rank.—*New York Evening Post.*

Profoundly interesting volume. It cannot be put aside as a collection of hurried conclusions of a careless student. Lavishly illustrated. Pages of deep interest relating to the stone-circles of Stonehenge and Keswick, discovering engraved marks previously overlooked by other observers. —*Daily Province*, Vancouver.

A stupendous thing. A book of Truth stranger than Fiction—written in a clear and straightforward style that appeals to the average intelligent reader who has an interest in progress and the manner of that progress of his race.—*Globe*, St. John, N.B.

The book is packed with interesting facts from the latest authorities, and the illustrations happily chosen. Indices are all that could be desired.—*Professor Sayce.*